CONTENTS

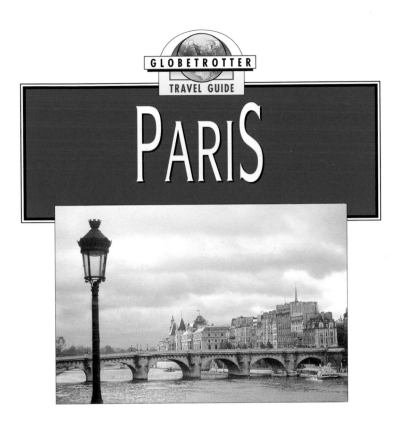

GLOBETROTTER
TRAVEL GUIDE

PARIS

MELISSA SHALES

NEW
HOLLAND

First published in 1996 by New Holland
(Publishers) Ltd
London • Cape Town • Sydney • Singapore

ISBN 1 85368 423 6

New Holland (Publishers) Ltd
24 Nutford Place, London W1H 6DQ

Commissioning Editor: Tim Jollands
Project Manager: Elizabeth Frost
Editor: Geraldine Christy
Editorial Assistant: Justine Brown
Design: Philip Mann, ACE Ltd
Cartography: Globetrotter Travel Maps/ML
Design, London

Typeset by Philip Mann, ACE Ltd
Reproduced in Singapore by P&W Graphics
PTE Ltd
Printed and bound in Hong Kong by South
China Printing Company (1988) Limited

Photographic credits: **David Alexander**, page 24;
Jacqui Cordingley, cover (top left), pages 23, 56
(top); **Peter Feeny**, title page, pages 6, 18, 95;
Brian Harding, pages 10, 107, 112; **Glenn
Harper**, pages 22, 96; **Roger Howard**, pages 19,
59, 62, 66, 105; **Hudson/Shales**, pages 7, 8, 40, 42,
44, 45, 46, 48, 49, 52, 56 (bottom), 57, 58, 71, 88
(top), 99; **Caroline Jones**, page 4; **Gordon
Lethbridge**, page 79; **David Lund**, pages 63, 82;
Norman Rout, pages 11, 35, 109, 111; **Melissa
Shales**, cover (bottom left), pages 12, 15, 16, 17,
20, 21, 30, 32, 34 (top and bottom), 37, 38, 43, 51,
65, 72, 74, 75, 80, 81, 83, 84, 87, 88 (bottom), 89,
90, 91, 93, 98, 102; **Stuart Spicer**, pages 9, 25, 33,
68; **Jeroem Snijders**, pages 26, 28, 29, 100 (top
and bottom), 101; **Chris Warren**, cover (top and
bottom right), pages 27, 55, 60, 67, 73, 76.

The author would like to thank the following
people for their generous assistance in the prepar-
ation of this book: Penelope Shales, who helped
enormously with expert knowledge of Paris and
all things French, lent me numerous books and
shot many of the photos for the book; Dennis
Hudson and Dominic Shales, who also helped
with pictures; Kirker European Travel, British
Midland, the Hôtel St Augustin and Disneyland
Paris who all helped with facilities.

Front cover photographs
Top left: *Notre Dame, viewed from across the Seine.*
Top right: *The influence of Art Nouveau is evident
in the original metro signs.* **Bottom right:** *The Eiffel
Tower, built for the 1889 Exhibition, now synony-
mous with Paris.* **Bottom left:** *Les Deux Magots,
well-known haunt of artists and writers, in St-
Germain.*

Title page photograph
*The Pont Neuf – or New Bridge – is, paradoxically,
the oldest in Paris.*

1
Introducing
Paris

A city of crowned heads and severed heads, with soaring architectural triumphs from the glorious Cathedral of Notre Dame to the magnificence of Versailles and the avant garde spectacle of the Georges Pompidou Centre, Paris is superb. Dramas, melodramas, great tragedies and comedies have all been enacted here, on and off the stage. The city has decided the fate of kings and empires and has nurtured many of the world's greatest artists, writers, philosophers and musicians. Every age has left a legacy of splendid monuments and gracious churches. Rulers of France, from Charles V to Napoleon III and President Mitterrand, have understood that their place in posterity is measured in stone, and Paris, more than any other European city, has a centuries-old, ongoing love affair with beautiful and innovative architecture. Yet the real magic of Paris comes not only from these magnificent creations, but from the shuttered, balconied boulevards, the winding backstreets, the small squares and the avenues of square-cut trees.

It is a city to be savoured slowly. Take comfortable shoes, decide on an area, then wander. Allow yourself time to enjoy the flower seller beside a tiny wrought-iron fountain, the brightly canopied pavement café rich with the smell of aniseed and fresh coffee, a subtly carved stone doorway, the statuesque mime artist perched on a concrete bollard. It is almost impossible to get lost. If your feet collapse under you, you will never be far from a metro. And if you haven't seen all the top ten sights, it doesn't really matter. They will still be there next time.

Opposite: *The Eiffel Tower seen from the Palais de Chaillot.*

Notre Dame dominates the Ile de la Cité in the midst of the Seine. The foundation stone of the cathedral was laid in 1163 by Pope Alexander III.

THE LAND

It is the works of man, not nature, that have given Paris its unique charm, yet the surrounding landscape, a low-lying plain in northern France, is gentle and fruitful with a light that has inspired generations of artists. The ancient Celts chose to build here for logistic and practical reasons. The river gave them excellent transport and a good supply of water and fish. The area is a natural trading crossroads and the islands were easily defended in a landscape virtually devoid of hilltops. It is still well situated for travel and transport throughout Europe.

Central Paris, defined by the terrifying ring road, the Boulevard Périphérique, covers a comparatively small area of about 105km^2 (40 sq miles) and has a population of around 2,250,000. It lies at the heart of the roughly circular Ile de France, which, in spite of its name, is not an island but defines the tiny area that was the personal domain of the early kings.

Today, the Ile de France, covering about 1200km^2 (460 sq miles), is made up of eight *départements*: Paris, Seine-et-Marne, Yvelines, Essonne, Hauts-de-Seine, Seine-St-Denis, Val-de-Marne and Val-d'Oise. Much of it is now effectively 'Greater Paris', covered by commuter towns and high-rise suburbs. With over 10 million inhabitants (a fifth of the country's population), it is the most densely populated region of France.

The Seine

Defining the geography, architecture and whole fibre of Paris, the River Seine loops slowly through the heart of the city for 12km (7^{1}/$_{2}$ miles), languidly accepting all tributes, including its recent elevation to World Heritage status. The river rises on the Langres Plateau, north-west of Dijon, and meanders gently across the country, moving slowly as it drops only 470m (1543ft) during its 774km (480 mile) journey from source to sea, at Le Havre on the Channel coast.

Paris, many miles inland, is still the fourth largest port in France (after Marseilles, Le Havre and Dunkirk) and the river is alive with traffic. The working docks are away from the centre in Gennevilliers and Charenton, but heavily laden barge trains groan slowly through the city, whole families living aboard; colonies of houseboats thrive along the banks; and a seemingly endless parade of sightseeing boats ply the river by day and night (see page 120), adding to the gaiety.

For nearly 2km (1^{1}/$_{4}$ miles) the river is bordered on both sides by double-decker quays, the earliest of which, the quai des Grands-Augustins, was built by Philip the Fair in 1313. Lined above by knobbly plane trees and below by cool, green poplars, the quays are wonderful for walking and picnics, although part of the right bank has now been usurped by a busy motorway. Through the city centre are also 36 bridges, the oldest, ironically called the Pont Neuf (New Bridge), opened in 1607 (see page 35). The most flamboyant , the Pont Alexandre III, with pillars surmounted by gilded statues, was built for the 1900 World Exhibition (see page 72).

THE ZOUAVE

The first Pont de l'Alma was built in 1856, to celebrate Napoleon II's victory in Crimea, but eroded so badly that a shiny new steel version was erected in 1972. Only one column of the old bridge remains, adorned by a statue of a Polish Second Empire soldier, now known as the Zouave. He has become the city's official bench mark, used to measure the height of the Seine in times of flood. The highest on record is when the water reached his chin in January 1910. He is best seen from a boat.

The Zouave on the Pont de l'Alma is on permanent sentry duty in case of flooding

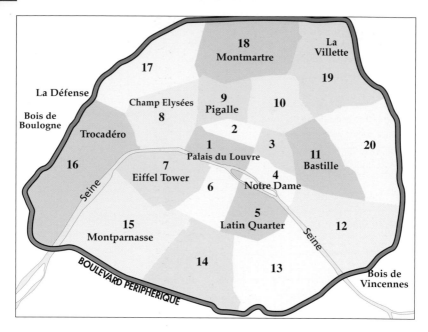

Traditional flower stalls are still a romantic option in this bustling modern city.

The Arrondissements

Nineteenth-century Paris was a lawless place, seething with rebellion, no matter who was in power. There was little chance of keeping control in the narrow, winding streets, so easily blockaded and so very difficult for moving troops. Napoleon III, aware of his tenuous grasp on power, determined to try to impose discipline on the unruly mob and on the very layout of the city. Between 1852 and 1870 his Prefect of the Seine, Baron Georges Haussmann, began to remodel Paris, literally sweeping away large sections of the city, sending over 200,000 poor people to live out of sight in a ring of shanty suburbs. On the Ile de la Cité alone 25,000 people were moved and throughout Paris thousands of homes and many outstanding buildings were demolished. The main streets were broadened and straightened, parks created, a proper underground sewer system constructed, and the opera house and railway stations built. From Haussmann's vision rose modern Paris, an elegant,

A bird's-eye view of the Jardins du Trocadéro and Palais de Chaillot seen from the Eiffel Tower.

bourgeois city of wide, tree-lined boulevards and open spaces, offering an uncluttered view of many of the major monuments.

Among the many buildings to tumble were the city walls, their space used to create a ring road, the Boulevard Périphérique. For the first time the whole area within this circle was incorporated into the Ville de Paris and the districts were redivided into 20 arrondissements. The system is still in use today, starting at the heart of Paris, the Louvre, with the first arrondissement, and spiralling out clockwise to the twentieth. Anything outside the Périphérique is counted as a suburb. This system makes it easy to learn your way around the city. All street signs and maps mark the arrondissement alongside the name.

THE SUBURBS

The suburbs have an odd mixture of styles and all seem rather unplanned, with 50-year-old villas next to soulless apartment blocks. La Défense is ultra-modern, Neuilly is elegant, St-Denis surrounds a great medieval basilica, while American-style houses squat oddly round the palace in the Versailles area. On the whole, the more elegant suburbs are to the west, the poorer areas to the east, although the advent of Disneyland Paris with its new facilities and excellent transport is beginning to shift the balance.

Street sign displaying the number of the arrondissement. Many streets are named after celebrated French men and women.

Arrondissement by Arrondissement

First Rich and royal Paris, with the Louvre, part of the Ile de la Cité, and serious shopping at the Forum des Halles and the Rue St Honoré.

Second The financial centre, surrounding the Bourse (Stock Exchange) and the Bibliothèque Nationale (National Library).

Third Delightfully villagey, with the narrow streets and grand mansions of part of the Marais.

Fourth One of the most beautiful in Paris, with the eastern half of the Ile de la Cité, Ile St Louis, the major part of the Marais, the Tour St Jacques, and Beaubourg (Georges Pompidou Centre).

Fifth Lively and entertaining, with the Latin Quarter, Roman and medieval Paris, and masses of students around the Sorbonne.

Sixth Vibrant street life with really good shopping and eating, around Boulevard Saint-Michel and Saint-Germain-des-Prés.

Seventh Monumental and grandiose, with the Eiffel Tower, the Hôtel des Invalides with its five museums and Napoleon's tomb, and the Assemblée Nationale.

Eighth Rich and glamorous, home of haute couture, the area round the Champs Elysées and Rue du Faubourg-St-Honoré.

Ninth The greatest concentration of hotels in Paris, best for affordable shopping and night life, from the department stores of the Grands Boulevards to the Pigalle cabarets.

Tenth The Gare du Nord and the Gare de l'Est. The Canal St Martin. A lot of red lights, working girls and boys.

Eleventh The Bastille, birthplace of revolution, now becoming young and trendy.

Twelfth Heading off the map into the Bois de Vincennes with its lakes and zoo.

Thirteenth Rather ugly modern Chinese and Vietnamese quarter with many good, cheap Chinese restaurants.

Fourteenth Best seen from underground, home to the Montparnasse Cemetery and the Catacombs.

Fifteenth Montparnasse, once home to artists and musicians and still a place of excess, with Tour Montparnasse, the highest tower in Paris, and rue Vaugirard – the longest street in the city (4360m [2^3/$_4$ miles]).

Sixteenth Très chic, très snob . . . Residential area around the Palais de Chaillot, with tall, elegant houses, inhabited by tall, elegant people, on long, elegant streets.

Seventeenth The Palais des Congrès. A residential area.

Eighteenth Tourist heaven, home of Montmartre, with charming bistros, bad artists, and excellent views.

Nineteenth The Parc de la Villette – revitalized as a techno-beacon with the Cité des Sciences et de l'Industrie.

Twentieth A non-area, surrounding the Père Lachaise Cemetery.

THE FRENCH

'The French character is indeed a character, stampt upon them from without. Their profoundest thoughts are bon mots. They are the only nation that ever existed, in which a government can be hist off the stage like a bad play, and in which its fall excites less consternation, than the violation of a fashion in dress.'
J. C. and A. Hare, *Guesses at Truth*, 1847.

Wrought-iron balconies in Montmartre have changed little since the artists made this quarter their own in the 19th century.

HISTORY IN BRIEF

The history of Paris is one of death from famine and disease amongst the poor, of ostentatious consumption amongst the rich, all stained by the blood of war and siege, riot and revolution. The city has been invaded or besieged by the Romans, Alemanni, Franks, Huns, Vikings, English and, several times, the Germans.

The gaps between were filled by home-grown violence, directed usually at an autocratic monarchy with little grasp of the real world. Almost all the turmoil that spread throughout France began with the Paris mob, who started not only the 1789 revolution but many others as well. As far back as 1270 and 1277, Parisians

The history of Paris is to a great extent the history of France, and the figure of the Emperor Napoleon towers over both. His exploits are commemorated throughout the city and he is buried impressively in Les Invalides.

held their first recorded general strikes, which resulted in King Louis IX setting up the first municipal council, run by the Guilds. In 1358 they stormed the palace and forced the Dauphin to grant a degree of parliamentary democracy – only for it to be revoked later the same year. The 19th century saw revolutions in 1830, 1848 and 1871; in the 20th century came the 'Student Revolt' of May 1968, which spread into many other strata of society and even across French borders.

Important Dates

*c*300BC Celtic Parisii tribe settle on the islands.

52BC Julius Caesar's troops defeat Gauls, who destroy the city. By the 1st century AD, the Romans have built a small but thriving new city, Lutetia.

AD256–80 First Barbarian invasions. City almost destroyed by Franks and Alemanni.

*c*262 St Denis, first Bishop of Lutetia, is martyred.

360 City name changed to Paris.

451 St Geneviève leads triumphant defence of Paris against Attila the Hun, and becomes its patron saint after her death in 512 (see page 91).

508 Frankish king, Clovis, defeats Romans. Paris becomes capital of the Christian Merovingian empire.

8th–9th century Paris becomes a backwater as Charlemagne moves his capital to Aix-la-Chapelle. Empire attacked by Normans (Vikings) in 845, 846 and 861.

885 Eudes, Count of Paris, repulses Norman siege and his heirs become the most powerful of the French lords.

987 Hugues Capet, is declared King of France, founding the Capetian dynasty.

1183 Peter Abélard and followers found the University of Paris.

1167 Opening of food market in Les Halles.

1215 The University of Paris eventually given official recognition.

1253 Sorbonne University founded.

1302 First meeting of the Estates General, France's closest answer to a parliament, made up of representatives of the nobility, clergy and commons.

*c*1310 Establishment of the Parlement de Paris as a judicial court.

1339 The Hundred Years War against England begins.

1348 Outbreak of plague kills over a third of the population.

1356 King Jean II is captured by the English, leaving France in anarchy.

PARIS FIRSTS

1534 St Ignatius Loyola founds the Society of Jesus (Jesuits) on Montmartre.

1783 First manned ascent in hot air balloon by Pilatre de Rozier and the Marquis d'Arlandes.

1818 Daguerre and Niepce invent photography.

1885 Louis Pasteur invents the principles of inoculation with rabies vaccine.

1895 Auguste and Louis Lumière invent the ciné camera and show the world's first movie. They also invent colour photography.

1898 Pierre and Marie Curie discover radium.

1983 Luc Montagnier isolates the AIDS virus.

1358 The Provost, Etienne Marcel, storms the palace with a mob, forcing the Dauphin, Charles V, to grant parliamentary democracy. Marcel is later killed, and all democratic rights are revoked.

1420 English king, Henry V, occupies Paris and claims throne of France.

1429 Unsuccessful siege, led by Joan of Arc.

1436 Charles VII recaptures an anarchic and virtually bankrupt Paris.

1528 François I moves from the Marais into the Louvre, which becomes a royal palace.

1562–98 The Wars of Religion between Catholics and Huguenots split France. Catherine de Medici arranges a truce, gathers Huguenot leaders in Paris and massacres them, together with over 10,000 other Protestants. War ends when Protestant king Henry IV (of Navarre) besieges Paris, converts to Catholicism to claim the throne, then signs the Edict of Nantes, guaranteeing freedom of worship.

1610–42 Reign of Louis XIII, assisted by Cardinal Richelieu, becomes a golden age of bourgeois prosperity and efficiency for the city.

1643–1715 Reign of Louis XIV, the megalomaniac 'Sun King', who nearly bankrupts the country by his lavish lifestyle, creates unworkably detailed laws, sets up a highly unpopular network of spies and overtaxes everyone. At the same time, his reign is a triumph of luscious, frothy music, art and theatre.

1648–60 Several small-scale rebellions against the king, including the Fronde.

1682 Entire court, including 10,000 aristocratic hangers-on, moves to Versailles.

1685 Louis revokes the Edict of Nantes.

1789 Start of the French Revolution (see page 15).

2 December 1804 Napoleon crowns himself Emperor in Notre Dame.

1814 Napoleon is exiled to Elba. Elderly Louis XVIII is restored to the throne.

1815 After his escape, Napoleon marches north. He is defeated for the last time at Waterloo and is exiled to St Helena, where he dies in 1821.

1830 The three-day revolution, Les Trois Glorieuses, topples ineffective Charles X, replacing him by a distant relative, Louis-Philippe.

1832 19,000 Parisians die in cholera epidemic.

1848 Revolution of Contempt leads to the Second Republic with Napoleon's nephew, Louis-Napoleon, as president.

1851 Louis-Napoleon declares himself Emperor Napoleon III. Start of Second Empire.

1852–70 Haussmann virtually rebuilds Paris (see page 8).

1870–71 The Franco–Prussian War. Napoleon is captured; radicals take over the Assemblée Nationale, declaring a Third Republic, based at Versailles. Paris is besieged by Germans; Parisians form themselves into a Committee of National Defence. They hold off the siege, but the Assemblée Nationale surrenders and Germans march into Paris. In the aftermath the Committee resists attempts to disarm it and forms the Paris Commune, which is eventually controlled after six weeks of bloody fighting with French government troops, leaving over 20,000 dead, another 25,000 imprisoned and

---

CALENDAR OF THE REVOLUTION

1784 The Farmers-General (tax-gatherers) persuade Louis XVI to build a new wall round an already distressed city, to help them collect entry tolls.

1789 With the country falling to pieces, Louis is persuaded to call the Estates General for the first time since 1614.

5 May The Estates convene at Versailles.

17 June The commons declare themselves a National Assembly and promise to give France a constitution before they stand down.

12 July Crowds attack the toll booths on the Farmers Wall.

14 July A mob storms the Bastille. Lafayette forms the Paris militia and designs the tricolour – with royal white and the red and blue of Paris.

November All church property is confiscated.

1790 Nobles and clergy renounce all their privileges.

1791 Royal family captured while attempting to escape Paris, and held as prisoners in the Tuileries.

10 August 1792 Crowds take the Louvre and the hardline Commune overthrows the relatively moderate government.

22 September A new *Convention Nationale* is elected and proclaims a Republic.

21 January 1793 Execution of Louis XVI ends 805 years of the monarchy. The severed head is displayed to the crowd.

2 June Communards overthrow the Convention and arrest moderate Girondins.

September Start of the Terror, led by Marat and Robespierre. 2600 people sent to the Guillotine.

27 July 1794 Robespierre himself is executed, ending the Terror. Power moves to a new five-man *Directoire*.

1799 Napoleon Bonaparte stages a successful coup, enticing the whole government to St Cloud for their protection and arresting them.

1804 Napoleon declares himself Emperor.

---

untold damage to the city. Paris loses any form of real self-government for the next 106 years.

1914 Paris escapes invasion during World War I after Battle of the Marne, as Paris taxi drivers rally to drive reserve troops to the front.

1919 Versailles Treaty ends World War I.

14 June 1940 Government flees, leaving Paris to be occupied by Nazis.

24 August 1944 Paris liberated. Allied troops hold back and the Free French under Leclerc lead the triumphant entry. De Gaulle arrives two days later.

May 1968 Student riots spread across the country.

1977 Jacques Chirac elected first mayor of Paris since 1871.

1989 Massive celebrations for the bicentenary of the Revolution.

The names of those who died in the three-day revolution of July 1830 are inscribed on the July Column in the Place de la Bastille.

THE GEOGRAPHY OF POWER

The **Palais de l'Elysée**, *55 rue du Faubourg-St-Honoré, 8th*, is the official residence of the President, while the Prime Minister lives in the **Hôtel Matignon**, *57 rue de Varenne, 7th*. The **Palais Bourbon**, *126 rue de l'Université, 7th*, is the seat of the Assemblée Nationale, while the Sénat meets in the **Palais du Luxembourg**, *15 rue de Vaugirard, 6th*. Paris is also the home of **UNESCO** (United Nations Educational, Scientific, and Cultural Organization), *7 place de Fontenoy, 7th*, and the **OECD** (Organization for Economic Co-operation and Development), *2 rue André Pascal, 16th*. Each of the 20 arrondissements has its own town hall, but the Mairie de Paris, the administrative centre of the city, is in the **Hôtel de Ville**, *4th*.

GOVERNMENT AND ECONOMY

Paris has been the capital of France for 2000 years and the politics of city and state are inexorably entwined. France is a republic, led by an executive President, who is elected for seven years and governs with the aid of a Prime Minister and cabinet. There are two houses of parliament; the law-making *Assemblée Nationale*, elected for five years, and the *Sénat*, with advisory powers only.

Internally, however, power in France is largely devolved to the provinces, with the country split into 22 regions, 96 départements and 36,532 communes. Each Paris arrondissement has its own council and administration, and the city as a whole is a département, under the auspices of the *Conseil de Paris*.

Paris Politics

Much of the violence and bloodshed in French history stems from the determination of Parisians to have greater freedom of self-government. The power of the mob has ebbed and flowed over the centuries and most rulers have feared its wrath, but the succession of revolutions in 1789, 1830 and 1848, followed swiftly by the 1871 Commune, became too much to take. All semblance of local government was dismantled and the city was brought under direct state control. It was 106

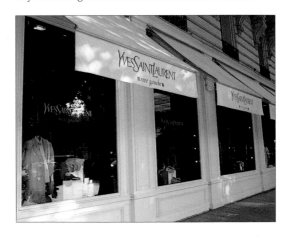

The understated chic of the fashion house Yves St Laurent prêt-à-porter, on the Rive Gauche.

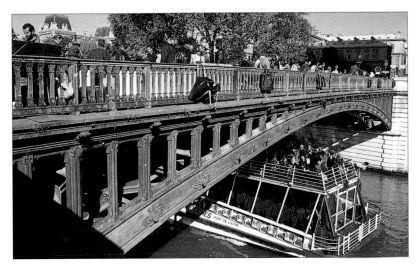

years before Paris finally regained a mayor in 1977, with the outspoken and politically ambitious Jacques Chirac. Almost from the moment he took office the struggle for control began again, but this time with monuments as weapons. The city became a giant Lego set as President and Mayor battled to create its most impressive building and most spectacular celebration.

A trip on a tour boat under the bridges of Paris is an ideal way to view the city's sights.

Economy

On the whole, all this rivalry has been good for the development of infrastructure. The city has been carefully restored, is well kempt and efficiently run – and it has some of the most exciting and innovative modern architecture in Europe. There has also been a massive boom in tourism, which is now the city's main money-spinner. There are some other money-making industries, most notably fashion, with the couturier houses as loss-leaders and spin-offs such as ready-to-wear and perfume making the money, while the surrounding Ile de France is heavily industrial. On the whole, however, central Paris feeds on itself and the rest of the country – a charming showcase of society and government, the arts and media.

CHIRAC

Born in 1932, Jacques René Chirac was elected to the Assemblée Nationale in 1967 and became Prime Minister in 1974. Two years later he resigned to form a breakaway Gaullist party. In 1977 he became Mayor of Paris, a position he held until 1995. He was unsuccessful in his bid for the Presidency in 1981. Ever optimistic, however, he stood again for the 1995 Presidential election and this time was successful in his challenge.

Above: Exclusive shops line the Place Vendôme.

Opposite: Feeding the birds in the Jardin des Tuileries.

BALLOONING

In 1783 word reached Paris of the Montgolfier brothers' experiment. Paris went balloon-crazy. Two months later, physicist Jacques Charles released the city's first, from the Place des Victoires. Shortly after that, Pilatre de Rozier and the Marquis d'Arlandes made the first manned ascent, flying 100m (330ft) from the Château de Muette to Butte-aux-Cailles.

For balloon flights today, contact **France Montgolfières sarl.**, tel: 40 60 11 23; or **Air Escargot**, tel: 16-85 87 12 30. For helicopter rides, contact **Héli-France**, tel: 45 54 95 11; **ABC Hélicoptères**, tel: 69 90 14 18; or **Paris Hélicoptère System**, tel: 48 35 90 44.

THE PEOPLE

Everyone knows the clichés – Parisians are haughty and unwelcoming, intellectually pretentious, appalling drivers and terrible snobs. Some are, of course. Certain types do still exist: the well-bred *haute bourgeoisie*, with their drawl and slightly old-fashioned chic; the old-style working class, who survive in small residential pockets in the city and can be seen buying food in the markets every day. However, the city is changing. Many people living in Paris today are immigrants, not only from provincial France, but from all over Europe, Africa and Asia. About the only truism left is that all Parisians *know* Paris is the centre of the civilized universe and barely recognize the existence of the rest of the world – except as a source of ingredients and for one month a year, during the August holiday, when they spill out of town *en masse* to the countryside and coast.

Religion

Although the church and state were formally separated in 1905, France is traditionally Catholic and most Parisians pay nominal service to the Church. Like most modern cities, however, few are devout and regular attendance at services is dropping. At the same time, the influx of North Africans has resulted in a growing Muslim population and there are also representatives of every other faith and cult somewhere in the city.

Lifestyle

Life in Paris is up-beat, fast-moving, exciting, invigorating, and totally exhausting. Parisians pride themselves on being sophisticated, highly educated and well read, on their broad-minded and tolerant attitude and their refusal to be shocked. They are enthusiastic theatre and cinema goers – egged on partly by the lamentable quality of French TV – are willing to discuss new ideas ad nauseam, and keep up a noble tradition of civil strife, strikes and demonstrations.

The city is young, and society driven by the wealthy and childfree. You see remarkably few small children around and few concessions are made to them. People are staying single longer and having families later and, with the improvements in public transport, there is a growing tendency for Parisians to move out to the suburbs when they start a family.

Image is all important, whether in clothes, car or the quality of the furniture. Even if the salon is a museum piece, the private rooms behind may well be scruffy. Fashion swings like a metronome, as people scurry towards the new trendy district or restaurant. In terms of clothes, street fashion is a very mixed bag and by no means all Parisians have chic, but the majority are probably making some sort of statement. There is a high level of cultural appreciation and Parisians enjoy discussing and philosophizing at length over innovation, especially in art and ideas. They do so, however, in an atmosphere that cherishes the style and decorative detail that has traditionally meant 'Paris' to the rest of the world.

LE VAU

Louis Le Vau (1612–70), the great French architect of the seventeenth century, was born in Paris. The son of a master mason and trained by his father, his skill first came to the fore in the 1640s when he designed a number of private houses for the wealthy on the Ile St Louis. He was then commissioned by Fouquet, Louis XIV's finance minister, to design the magnificent château of Vaux-le-Vicomte (see page 110). His great talents recognized, Le Vau was appointed to work on the Louvre, but it was at Versailles (see page 104) where his abilities ran full rein. There he assembled an unsurpassable team of decorators, painters, sculptors and gardeners to produce the most splendid of palaces for the Sun King.

THE ARTS
Architecture

The mid-12th-century foundation of Notre Dame (1163) and the Sainte-Chapelle (1245) heralded in the great era of Gothic architecture that seemed to spring fully fledged and triumphant from the narrow, grimy streets of Paris. It was such a success that the city largely ignored Italy's return to classical elegance and only caught up with the Renaissance in the late 16th century with the rebuilding of the Louvre (1546–59) and the Place des Vosges (1605–12). Even so, it scarcely paused for breath before sweeping on to the Baroque, epitomized by the lavish flamboyance of Versailles (1661–82), and an era

Right: *The colonnade in the courtyard of the Palais Royal provides a contrasting backdrop for a modern steel sculpture by Daniel Buren.*

Opposite: *The tomb of Voltaire, the leading philosophical writer of the 18th-century Enlightenment, in the Panthéon.*

dominated by the architect Le Vau (1612–70), painter Le Brun (1619–90) and landscape gardener Le Nôtre (1613–1700). Variations on this gilded glamour and fussiness remained popular right into the 20th century, with several destructive puritanical interludes.

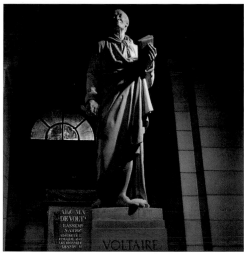

The Napoleons added a new sombre tone to the streets with massive, Imperial neo-classical buildings such as the Arc de Triomphe (1806–14 and 1832–6). The Great Exhibitions (see page 83) brought in experimental triumphs in iron and glass, such as the Eiffel Tower (1889) and riotous art nouveau Grand Palais and Pont Alexandre III (both 1896–1900). The post-war era has seen an exciting new boom in innovative design, with projects such as the Georges Pompidou Centre (1977), the Louvre Pyramid (1988) and the Grande Arche de La Défense (1989).

Words

The intellectuals, and pseudo-intellectuals, of Paris have long regarded ideas as entertainment and words as sexy, lionizing philosophers from Abélard in the 12th century (see page 51) to the 20th-century Existentialists.

In 1635, Cardinal Richelieu founded the *Académie Française*, with its closed membership and closed minds, that has stripped thousands of words from the French language in the name of purity, leaving it much the poorer. The real golden age of French literature began as a frippery, in the resplendent court of Louis XIV, where many bored, wealthy nobles needed constant entertaining to stop them plotting rebellion. The resultant outpouring of fine drama was headed by Molière (1622–73), whose acid comedies of manner

(see page 83)
(see page 51)

THE COMEDIE-FRANCAISE

France's first national theatre, the Comédie-Française, has the official title of Le Théâtre Français. It was founded in 1680 by Louis XIV and brought together two Paris theatre companies, the Hôtel de Bourgogne (itself an amalgamation of the Théâtre du Marais with Molière's own company) and the Théâtre Guénégaud. With a royal grant the company enjoyed a number of privileges, but they were abolished during the Revolution and the theatre disbanded. Later re-established, it was granted a decree by Napoleon in 1812. The company has performed the works of all the great French dramatists, notably the plays of Corneille, Molière and Racine.

delighted the very people they satirized; and Corneille (1606–84) and Racine (1639–99), whose broad range of poetic tragedy and comedy is ranked alongside Shakespeare.

Two authors dominate the 18th century: Voltaire (1694–1778), author of outspoken ironic novels and short stories; and Beaumarchais (1732–99), whose works, *The Barber of Seville* and *The Marriage of Figaro,* were transformed into Mozart's finest operas. Other philosophical writers of the time were Rousseau (1712–78), whose work *Emile* opened up the debate on education; and Diderot (1713–84), whose Encyclopedia brought together numerous contributors in an attempt to set down a rational explanation for the universe. The 19th century saw a new flowering of literary genius amongst the city's novelists and poets, including the flamboyant Balzac (1799–1850); the romantics – Victor Hugo (1802–85), George Sand (1804–76), and Gustave Flaubert (1821–80); tragic Baudelaire (1821–67); the dry, moralist Emile Zola (1840–1902) and, introspective Marcel Proust (1871–1922).

In the 1920s and 30s numerous eminent British and American authors, including Henry Miller, Ernest Hemingway, Gertrude Stein and George Orwell, headed for the Paris cafés. Depression and war interrupted the flow of ideas and alcohol, but both were revived in the 1950s with the advent of the Existentialists Sartre, de Beauvoir and Camus, who made their home from home in *Les Deux Magots* in St-Germain.

Since then, the banner has been taken up by somewhat esoteric authors such as Alain Robbe-Grillet and Nathalie Sarraute, but Paris is still waiting for a new flowering of talent that will grip the world.

OVER COFFEE

Café society flourished in 18th-century Paris. The cafés were places to meet friends, drink coffee and discuss politics or literature. Perhaps the most famous of them all was the Café Procope at no 13 rue de l'Ancienne-Comédie. Here the *philosophes* would gather to debate at leisure. Voltaire was a frequent visitor and it is said that Diderot and d'Alembert first thought up the idea for their Encyclopedia here.

Music

Astonishingly, in spite of the superb Conservatoire and Opéra, Paris had little influence on music until the mid-19th century, mainly producing only frothy entertainment, with some honourable exceptions such as Lully (1632–87) and Gluck (1714–87), both of whom were foreign. Parisian Berlioz (1803–69) was forced to work abroad. As with the other arts, Parisian music reached its zenith in the 19th century when composers such as Rossini (1792–1868), Chopin (1810–49), Liszt (1811–86), Wagner (1813 83), Offenbach (1819–80), César Franck (1822–90), Saint-Saëns (1835–1921), Fauré (1845–1924), Debussy (1862–1918) and Ravel (1875–1937) flocked into the city, along with Diaghilev's Russian ballet. At the same time popular nightlife was becoming increasingly important. Possibly the city's greatest home-grown contribution has been to cabaret, sparked by the glamorous, high-kicking chorus line of the can-can (1830, to music by Offenbach), eventually producing singers such as Maurice Chevalier and Edith Piaf, and showcasing the great foreigners, Josephine Baker and Marlene Dietrich.

Paint and Canvas

In the Middle Ages the finest Parisian art was in the stones, glorious stained glass, exquisite reliquaries and illuminated manuscripts of the churches. Secular work was confined largely to furniture and Gobelin tapestries which doubled as central heating. However, during his unsuccessful wars in Italy, François I (1494–1547) discovered the High Renaissance, returning to Paris with Leonardo da Vinci and carts piled high with fine art. His

Above: *The art of mime thrives in Paris and street performers enliven the areas around Montmartre and Beaubourg.*

Opposite: *The Polish-born composer Chopin spent much of his life in Paris and is buried in Père-Lachaise cemetery.*

THE IMPRESSIONISTS

The Impressionist painters delighted in conveying light and atmosphere, enjoying colour for its own sake. As a group of artists they are individual in style, but are linked by their interest in painting directly from nature and in developing the theories of harmonious and complementary colour. Inspired by Manet's exhibition of 1863 (see page 82) and disillusioned with the established academic attitude to art, they held their first joint exhibition in 1874. The name came from Monet's painting *Impression, Sunrise* and was used as an umbrella term by a critic to deride the group. There were eight Impressionist exhibitions in all and the painters exhibiting in each varied, though those involved included Monet, Renoir, Sisley, Pissarro, Cézanne, Degas and Morisot.

successors grasped the idea but not the quality and Parisian art settled back into fluffy decoration, propagandist statues and second-rate portraits, with delightful exceptions such as the delicate and romantic works of Watteau (1684–1721), Boucher (1703–70) and Fragonard (1732–1806).

Revolution and the 19th century saw a complete change, as artists such as Corot (1796–1875) and Delacroix (1798–1863) took to the streets, painting the scenes around them and infusing their work with a new depth while maintaining a deft touch with exquisite use of light and richness of colour. They opened a floodgate of new ideas and experimentation that has changed the course of artistic history.

Paris now became home to the greatest gathering of artistic talent since Renaissance Florence as artists flocked to the city from all over France. The roll-call is stupendous – Pissarro (1830–1903), Manet (1832–83), Degas (1834–1917), Cézanne (1839–1906), Rodin (1840–1917), Monet (1840–1926), Renoir (1841–1919), Rousseau (1844–1910), Gauguin (1848–1903), Van Gogh (1853–90), Seurat (1859–91) and Toulouse-Lautrec (1864–1901), to name but a few. Ideas flourished, with

Parisians enjoy sculpture in the open air. This bronze statue of a female nude is in the Jardin des Tuileries.

Urban art flourishes in Paris and the spray-can painter makes the most of any available space.

Impressionism, Pointillism, Fauvism and Expressionism. Paris rejected them all, however, and most of these great artists lived in abject poverty throughout their lives.

With the new century came Cubism and Surrealism and a new crop of superb artists, including Matisse (1869–1954), Mondrian (1872–1944), Epstein (1880–1959), Léger (1881–1955), Picasso (1881–1973), Braques (1882–1963), Utrillo (1883–1955), Modigliani (1884–1920), Chagall (1887–1985), Ernst (1891–1976) and Miró (1893–1983). Until the outbreak of World War II it became crucial for any serious artist to study in Paris. Today the city is still actively sponsoring new work, but the artistic community is more fragmented and, thanks to air travel, we are unlikely ever again to see such a concentration of talent in one city.

CINEMA

Since Auguste and Louis Lumière opened the world's first cinema in Paris in 1895, the city has remained the centre of a small but steady French film industry that has produced several of the world's finest film-makers, including Jean Renoir (son of the painter), Abel Gance, Marcel Pagnol, Jean Cocteau, Jacques Tati, François Truffaut, Jean-Luc Goddard and Louis Malle, and some of the world's favourite stars, such as Maurice Chevalier, Charles Boyer, Jean-Paul Belmondo, Simone Signoret, Brigitte Bardot, Jeanne Moreau, Gérard Dépardieu, Catherine Deneuve and Alain Delon.

FOOD AND DRINK

Parisians appear obsessed by food. The city is the gastronome's heaven, the spiritual and physical home of haute cuisine, with possibly the greatest concentration of fine food in the world. However, all is not as rosy as it might seem in Paradise.

The State of the Art

French eating habits are changing. Most women now work and simply do not have the time to cook long, luscious meals; busy, cholesterol-aware office workers are shunning the traditional three-course lunch in favour of a quick snack at their desk; and supermarkets are squeezing out many smaller shopkeepers. Everyday food is much simpler than before, with frozen and vacuum-packed ingredients common and a booming trade in ready-prepared meals. These are usually traditional dishes such as *cassoulet* or *coq au vin*, but the spectacular success of Marks and Spencer's food hall has created a new vogue for chilli con carne and lemon meringue pie.

All this change, tragically, has begun to filter through into the restaurants and cafés and you can no longer be assured of quality. There are still delightful traditional restaurants and chic new bistros with imaginative young chefs. But there are also many corner-cutting brasseries serving unimaginative, microwaved food, who rely on a flashy shopfront and gullible passing tourists to fill their coffers.

Take the weight off your feet, sip a drink and simply watch the world go by at a pavement café.

The Internal Clock

A typical French breakfast is tea, milky coffee or hot chocolate with a croissant or baguette and jam. Many hotels, used to international visitors, may add the choice of ham and cheese, fruit juice and yoghurt.

Lunch can be a simple snack or a full meal. Go early, as restaurants begin to fill up from 12 noon onwards. If on a limited budget, consider eating your main meal at midday as the fixed price lunch menus are excellent value, while a light snack, such as an omelette and salad, can be horribly expensive. Some places, however, also do a good value one-course *plat du jour*. Alternatively, the best option is to picnic. The key ingredients – bread, paté, cheese, sausage and fruit – are all easily available, as are bottled water, wine and cans of soda. Many delicatessens also sell ready-made salads, quiches, made-up sandwiches and pizza. Ferocious signs forbid you to sit on any grass, but there are plenty of benches and fountain steps, and the quays beside the Seine are excellent picnic spots.

Dinner begins surprisingly early, at about 19:00. Do not arrive much after 21:00 or everything will be full. Ideally, it is safer to reserve in advance. Eating after the

In many areas of Paris there are still traditional shops that sell wines, delicious honeys, jams and conserves, teas, chocolate and savoury delicacies.

theatre or opera is not easy, unless you go 'ethnic' or to the more bohemian areas of the Left Bank. Again, most restaurants have a range of two- or three-course set menus at different prices, all of which are cheaper than the à la carte options. Some also include wine and coffee.

Bistro or Brasserie

The range and sheer number of restaurants in Paris is overwhelming. Choosing where to eat can be one of the greatest pleasures of your holiday (see Paris At a Glance, page 116). A few top restaurants are so obviously famous that you have to book months in advance, and probably take out a large bank loan. For a good, relatively cheap meal, select an area, then wander the side streets, reading menu boards outside until you find one that makes you salivate. Avoid those with too long a menu. Food is likely to be fresher and cooked specially for you with only a limited number of dishes on offer. The 1st arrondissement, just behind the Louvre, has many excellent options at a higher price. For cheaper meals, the best hunting areas are Montmartre/Pigalle, and the Latin Quarter.

The café/bar serves drinks, coffee and light snacks such as *croque monsieur* (toasted ham and cheese sandwich) or *assiette anglaise* (assortment of salamis and cold meats) all day. It is always cheaper to stand at the

Fresh farmhouse cheeses from every part of France are sold in the heart of the city.

bar than to sit at a table and it may be even more expensive to sit at one of the premium pavement tables.

The brasserie originally started life as a beerhouse but has grown over the years into another form of eatery. Brasseries serve a basic menu of simple food such as *steak frites* (steak and chips), shellfish, omelettes, sausage *andouillette* (tripe sausage) and *choucroute* (sauerkraut) – and, of course, different beers. They serve food all day and usually have a reasonably priced set meal to keep you going.

The 'bistrot' was named in 1917 by White Russian emigrés (the word is Russian for 'quick'). Bistros began life as the Parisian fast food joints, small, cheap and cheerful restaurants serving a limited menu of hearty, unpretentious food. In their present form, they are still small and cheerful, with a slightly more ambitious menu and wine list and, usually, with a bar attached.

The interior of this art nouveau café retains its decorative detail and recalls the atmosphere of the giddy, social 1890s.

Ethnic Options

Cheaper French restaurants tend to have remarkably similar menus. However, the city is also home to an amazing array of other ethnic cuisines, brought by Russian and Polish refugees, immigrants from Greece and Italy, and former colonials from North Africa, China and Vietnam. Alongside these are Thai, Japanese and Indian restaurants and even English and Irish pubs. Many of these are excellent, offer extraordinarily good value, are one of few viable options for vegetarians and can be a welcome change from another *steak au poivre*.

2
The Islands

ILE DE LA CITE ***
(metro: Cité, Pont Neuf, St Michel)
The Conciergerie
Along the northern Quai de l'Horloge, the formidable **Conciergerie** began life as the 4th-century home of the Roman governor and 6th-century royal palace of Merovingian King Clovis. It remained the centre of government until 1358, after which the southern half, the **Palais de Justice**, became the home of parliament and the Supreme Court, while the northern half, the Conciergerie, housed the Concierge (Keeper of the Keys – a powerful politician whose duties included levying taxes) and the city prison. Amongst the earliest surviving buildings are the 13th-century Tour Bonbec (Babblers Tower), site of the torture chamber, and the Tour de l'Horloge, its public clock first installed in 1370.

Come the Revolution, the fortress entered its darkest and bloodiest period. In 1793–4 alone, during the worst days of the Terror, some 2600 people were imprisoned here on their way to the Guillotine, amongst them Queen Marie-Antoinette, Madame du Barry, Charlotte Corday (who stabbed Marat in his bath), and Citizens Danton and Robespierre. In a railed-off area, called the Rue de Paris, the prisoners of the Revolution were kept crowded together, sleeping on straw, being too poor to bribe their warders for better conditions. The guided tour takes you through several fine medieval halls, the kitchens, the executioner's apartments and the cells, including that of Marie-Antoinette.

The Islands

DON'T MISS

*** The Cathedral of Notre Dame
*** The Sainte-Chapelle:
two of the finest examples of Gothic architecture in the world.

Opposite: *The west (main) portal of the cathedral of Notre Dame shows the figure of Christ on its pier and sculptures representing the Last Judgment in the tympanum above.*

The Sainte-Chapelle ★★★

The lower chapel of the exquisite Sainte-Chapelle, used by the royal servants, is a masterpiece of vaulting.

In the 19th century the Palais de Justice was rebuilt, along with the French legal system. Virtually hidden by its high walls is the gemlike Sainte-Chapelle, built in 1246–8 by architect Pierre de Montreuil for saintly King Louis IX (1226–70) to house Christ's Crown of Thorns and other spectacular relics the king had retrieved from Venetian pawnbrokers. Some were lost during the Revolution, but those saved are now in Notre Dame and the slender, filigree building is more museum than church, with Mass celebrated only on 10 May, feast of St Yves, patron saint of lawyers. At ground-floor level is the servants' chapel, its sumptuous paintwork a product of 19th-century restoration. The upper royal chapel, a soaring triumphant kaleidoscope of stained glass linked together by fragile, fluted columns, is without doubt one of the world's most glorious architectural achievements.

The scene of many royal weddings, it was here in 1396 that Richard II of England was betrothed to Isabella, daughter of Charles VI of France.

Cathedral of Notre Dame ***

The magnificent cathedral, another Gothic masterpiece, is the culmination of numerous temples to pagan Cernunnos, guardian of the underworld, Roman Jupiter, and several Christian churches. Built between 1163 and 1330, it is 130m (425ft) long, with 69m (223ft) towers. The spire, added by 19th-century restorer Viollet-le-Duc, along with the splendid gargoyles of the *Galerie des Chimières* and green copper roof statues, is 90m (300ft) high.

The superb early 13th-century west façade begins with three arches, dedicated to the Virgin (left), St Anne (right), and the Last Judgment (centre). Above is the *Galerie des Rois d'Israel*, ancestors of Christ, and above that are Adam and Eve and the Virgin, surrounded by angels. It is possible to climb the 387 steps of the North Tower to see the bells, roofs, gargoyles and superb views over Paris.

There are three rose windows, each 13m (43ft) in diameter. The oldest and finest, in the north transept, was donated by St Louis in the 13th century and depicts Old Testament figures surrounding the Virgin. The south

The rose windows in Notre Dame have inspired generations of craftsmen.

GLORIOUS GLASS

The Sainte-Chapelle has nearly 1500m² (16,000 sq ft) of stained glass in 15 massive windows containing 1100 separate scenes. Of these, about 750 are 13th-century originals, the oldest in Paris. The others are superb 19th-century copies. The rose window, telling the story of Revelations, was added by Charles VIII in 1485. Together, they make up a pictorial bible. To read them, start in the lower left-hand corner and read left to right, travelling upwards.

Above: *A view of Notre Dame from the Square Jean XXIII shows the distinctive flying buttresses.*

Below: *The Wallace fountain in the Rue Lépine on the Ile de la Cité.*

rose, which is heavily restored, is dedicated to the New Testament, surrounding Christ in Majesty. The view of the west window, over the main door, is partially blocked by the magnificent organ, one of the largest in the world, with 108 stops and 7500 pipes.

Inside, tiny side chapels, many of them sponsored by medieval guilds, surround the towering nave. Through the centre a magnificent 14th-century carved screen, depicting the Nativity (north) and Resurrection (south), separates the ambulatory from the choir. The choir itself was rebuilt in 1723, honouring a vow made by Louis XIII. At the top is a beautiful pietà by Nicolas Coustou, flanked by marble Louis XIII and XIV. A door in the south wall opposite leads to the Treasury, a rich collection of gold and silver reliquaries, ivory figures, books and historical memorabilia.

Parvis du Notre Dame

The original square was a quarter of the size of today's vast, echoing Parvis du Notre Dame, created by Baron Haussmann in the mid-19th century (see page 8). A brass star set into the pavement just in front of Notre Dame marks **Point Zéro**, the exact point from which all distances in France are measured. On the left, the massive **Hôtel Dieu** has been the city's main hospital since AD660; to the right is the **Préfecture de Police**, site of a ferocious four-day battle between the police and German soldiers during the 1944 liberation of Paris.

In 1965 developers building a car park under the Parvis found a fascinating slice of history, with Roman and medieval walls and streets, the Merovingian cathedral and an 18th-century Foundlings Hospital. These are now preserved in the **Crypte Archéologique du Parvis de Notre Dame**, a beautifully presented underground museum that makes perfect sense of the maze of broken walls.

Other Sights

The charming **Place Dauphine** and the green and peaceful **Square du Vert Galant** named 'gay old spark' after the rollicking, womanizing king, Henry IV (of Navarre) once formed a separate islet, the Ile de Juif, used for burning Jews and witches, amongst them the Templar Grand Master, Jacques de Molay. The original equestrian statue of Henry IV was melted during the Revolution. This copy was made from the toppled statue of Napoleon which once graced the Vendôme Column! Nearby, the **Pont Neuf** is the oldest surviving bridge in Paris, opened in 1607 and, until the Revolution, the fashionable place to stroll and be seen.

A cool green daily flower market in **Place Louis-Lépine** gives way to a chattering bird market on Sunday mornings. Behind the cathedral are a small museum dedicated to its history, the **Musée de Notre Dame**, *10 rue du Cloître Notre Dame, 4th*, and the little tree-lined **Square du Jean XXIII**, site of the Bishop's Palace (destroyed by rioters in 1831), which offers superb views of the gloriously complex flying buttresses and statues which adorn the outside of the cathedral.

The eastern tip of the island is dedicated to the simple, but highly emotive modern **Memorial des Martyrs et de la Déportation**, dedicated to the 200,000 Frenchmen and women who died in Nazi labour and concentration camps during World War II.

> **A TURBULENT LIFE**
>
> Over the years, Notre Dame has seen the coronations of Henry VI of England (1430) and Napoleon Bonaparte (1804); thanksgiving services to celebrate the liberation of Paris from the English (1437) and the Germans (1944). During the Revolution it was badly damaged, renamed the Temple of Reason, with a local ballerina as goddess, and only narrowly escaped demolition thanks to the timely publication of Victor Hugo's novel, *The Hunchback of Notre Dame* (1831). It was further damaged in 1871 when Communards set it ablaze, changed their minds, but mistaking the Gallery of Kings of Israel and Judea on the façade for Kings of France, settled for lopping their heads off.

The Pont Neuf, the oldest bridge in Paris, connects the Ile de la Cité with both banks of the Seine.

ILE ST LOUIS WALK

Start at metro Pont Marie.
Cross the bridge and turn left
onto Quai d'Anjou. Turn right
past Square Barye, and right
again onto Quai de Béthune.
Take the first right, then first
left onto Rue St-Louis-en-l'Ile.
At Rue des Deux Ponts, turn
left, then right onto Quai
d'Orléans. Follow this round
to the Pont St Louis, then
turn right onto Rue St-Louis-
en-l'Ile. Back at Rue des Deux
Ponts, turn left for Pont
Marie and the metro.

ST LOUIS

Born in 1214, King Louis IX
succeeded to the throne at
the age of 12. The years of
regency under his mother led
to rebellion among the feudal
nobility, but once he had
taken over the government
Louis established legal and
administrative reforms and
promoted wider education.
He fought in the Crusades,
brought back many holy
relics to France, and was
responsible for the building
of Sainte-Chapelle and the
Sorbonne. Louis is revered for
his sense of justice and his
personal piety and religious
devotion. He died in Tunis
from the plague.

ILE ST LOUIS **

(metro: Pont Marie, Cité, Sully Morland)

Extraordinarily, Ile St Louis was virtually uninhabited
until the 17th century, used only for laundry, fishing and
grazing. Charles V (1364–80) dug a defensive canal along
the line of modern Rue Poulletier, creating two small
islands, Ile Notre Dame and Ile aux Vaches. In 1627, as
building boomed in the nearby Marais, an architect,
Christophe Marie, and two financiers, Poulletier and le
Regrattier, obtained a 60-year lease, permission to rejoin
the two islands and the rights to sell building land. They
laid out the basic grid of streets, surrounded the island by
tree-lined quays and encouraged the noble and wealthy to
buy. The resulting residential area has great elegance,
enormous charm, a permanent population of around 6000,
and feels as peaceful as a Sunday afternoon in the park.

There are few real sights. Instead, amble gently
through the narrow streets and round the tranquil quays
shaded by rustling poplar trees, breathe in the atmosphere and admire the detail on the many fine classical
hôtels. Many of the houses have plaques that name their
illustrious inhabitants, who include bankers, politicians,
artists, sculptors, writers and poets. The **Quais de
Bourbon** and **d'Anjou**, were originally *the* place to live. A
plain façade hides the lusciously decorative interior of the
Hôtel de Lauzun, *17, quai d'Anjou, 4th* (open at weekends). Built in 1657 for a financier who was sent to prison
before he could move in, the house is named after the
Duke of Lauzun, who commanded the French at the
Battle of the Boyne. Among the artists involved in its decoration were Le Brun, Le Sueur and Bourdon. Gautier,
Baudelaire, Rilke, Sickert and Wagner all lived here,
while in the 1840s it became home to the popular *Club des
Haschischins* (Hashish Eaters' Club), run by a famous
prostitute, Aglaë-Apollonie Sabatier. The cartoonist
Daumier lived at no 9 on the Quai d'Anjou. At the foot of
the island is a peaceful little park, the **Square Barye**,
named after another local inhabitant, an animal sculptor.

The southern **Quais d'Orléans** and **de Béthune** are
now the more fashionable address. The Quai d'Orléans

offers fine views over the flying buttresses of Notre Dame, and Landowski's elongated 1928 statue of St Geneviève (see page 91) on the **Pont de la Tournelle**. At no 6 are the Polish Library and the **Musée Adam-Mickiewicz**, with exhibits on Chopin and Mickiewicz, founder of the Polish Romantic movement.

Through the centre runs the main commercial **Rue St-Louis-en-l'Ile**. Halfway along, the Baroque **Church of St-Louis-en-l'Ile** (1664–1726) was designed by Le Vau. It has an elaborately gilded interior, a striking iron clock and an extraordinary spire, pierced by ovals, built in 1765 to replace the original which was burnt by lightning. Classical music concerts are regularly held here.

The Quai de Béthune on the Ile St Louis offers a relaxed walk by the river and a good view towards Notre Dame.

Le Vau also built **Hôtel Lambert** at no 2 *Rue St Louis-en-L'Ile*, which later became the home of Voltaire and Mme du Châtelet.

No 51, the delightful Rococo **Hôtel Chenizot**, was the home of Theresia Cabarrus in the 1790s. Nicknamed *Notre Dame de Thermidor*, she had eleven illegitimate children and was said to have slept with virtually the entire Revolutionary government. No 31 is the home of **Berthillon**, whose marvellous ice cream is a Parisian institution. The **Pont St-Louis**, across to the Ile de la Cité, is the ninth on the site; the site was cursed by gipsies in 1472 and the first bridge collapsed the day it was opened in 1634, drowning 20 people.

3
Beaubourg, Les Halles, the Marais and Bastille

THE RIVER

If the Ile de la Cité was the heart of royal and religious Paris, the right bank was undoubtedly the commercial centre. **La Samaritaine**, *19 rue de la Monnaie, 1st (metro: Pont Neuf)*, was opened in 1869 by a successful local merchant, Ernest Cognac, and named after a statue which stood under the arches of the Pont Neuf (see page 35). Today, it is one of the largest department stores in the city, with a superb art nouveau staircase and rooftop café which offers possibly the finest view in Paris.

The **Place du Louvre** *(metro: Louvre, Pont Neuf)* was once the headquarters of the Roman general, Labienus. The church of **St Germain l'Auxerrois**, first built in the 6th century, was fortified by the Normans and rebuilt as a collegiate church in 1025. From the 14th to the 19th century it became the royal chapel, and during the Revolution it even did duty as a gunpowder factory, police station and granary. In 1572 its bell was rung to mark the start of the St Bartholomew's Day Massacre (see page 14). The free-standing 19th-century belfry next door has an infinitely superior carillon of 38 bells, with regular recitals.

The **Place du Châtelet** stands on the site of a notoriously sinister medieval prison; underneath it is the world's largest metro station *(Châtelet-Les Halles)*. Just to the north is the beautiful 16th-century **Tour St Jacques**. This 52m (171ft) belfry is all that remains of the Eglise de St Jacques de la Boucherie, built by the Butchers' Guild at the official starting point of the pilgrim route to Santiago de Compostela in Spain.

DON'T MISS

*** **Centre Georges Pompidou**: France's national gallery of modern art in a mould-breaking building
*** **The Marais**: walk the streets and alleys of this delightful old quarter and visit the Place des Vosges, the Musée Picasso and the Musée Carnavalet.

Opposite: *This massive sculptured head complements the elegant gargoyles of St-Eustache.*

STRIKES, GIBBETS AND BONFIRES

Until Baron Haussmann changed its name, the peaceful Place de l'Hôtel de Ville was called the Place de Grève. It was the traditional place to find work; 'to do the grève' meant to be out of work. Gradually, the word came to be used for a strike.

It was also a place of execution, with regular public beheadings, hangings and burnings. In 1793, at the start of the Terror, the Guillotine was moved here. Over the next 18 months, it became a human abattoir, drenched with the blood of 2600 victims. Robespierre, the architect of the bloodshed, was arrested here in 1794 and guillotined.

Municipal government in Paris has been centred on the **Place de l'Hôtel de Ville** since 1260. The first **Hôtel de Ville** proper was designed under François I, but only completed in the 17th century. It became the headquarters of the Paris Commune throughout the Revolution and the Third Republic was declared here in 1870. The following year the building was torched by irate Communards (see page 15). The current splendid building only dates from 1874–82, although the central panel is a copy of the Renaissance hôtel.

LES HALLES *

rue Berger, rue Rambuteau, 1st (metro: Châtelet-Les Halles)

Les Halles opened for business in about 1110. By 1183 Philippe-Auguste had commissioned the first permanent market hall and was collecting rent and tax from an ever-growing number of stall holders selling everything from offal to gold lace. In 1851 Victor Baltard designed a new expandable hall of glass and green iron 'umbrellas'. In

1969 the fruit and vegetable market moved to hygienic, high-tech premises in the southern suburbs. By 1977 only a few street names were left to mark its passing, although the trendy have continued to come here to eat pigs' trotters and onion soup after the clubs close.

By 1979 a mushroom-topped modern complex sprouted from the gaping hole. Largely underground, it is mainly a busy, cavernous but uninspiring shopping mall with some small museums for the hardened sightseer. On Level 1 the **Musée Grévin** uses waxworks and audio-visuals to re-create turn-of-the-century Paris, while the **Musée Holographique** has a fantastic range of holographic images. The **Parc Océanique Cousteau** has

1. Centre Georges Pompidou
2. Fontaine des Innocents
3. Hôtel de Ville
4. Les Halles
5. Musée Carnavalet
6. Musée Cognacq-Jay
7. Musée des Instruments Musicales Mécaniques
8. Musée Picasso
9. Place des Vosges
10. Place Igor Stravinsky

more audio-visuals, concentrating on life under the ocean wave as seen by France's marine superstar, Jacques Cousteau. The **Vidéothèque de Paris**, *2 Grande Galerie*, offers an enormous array of film and television images, all featuring Paris, dating back to 1895.

On the whole, the large park on the roof is the best bit of the new complex. Broken into distinct areas by canopied walkways and pavilions, it has a fine children's playground and several interesting modern sculptures. The western end is marked by the circular **Bourse du Commerce**, the former granary exchange, beside which is a free-standing column once used by Catherine de Medici and her astrologers (including Nostradamus) as a platform for plotting the stars.

Opposite: *St-Eustache framed by the ironwork of the Jardin des Halles, created when the market moved out of town.*

With the Place Igor Stravinsky Paris celebrates the music of the Russian composer with joyful water sculptures.

The crowning glory, however, is the view across sculptor Henri de Miller's huge stone head to the vast **Eglise de St-Eustache**. The first 13th-century church was built by a merchant made wealthy by market concessions. The existing high Gothic church (1532–1640) was modelled on Notre Dame, with an oddly disparate neo-classical façade added in 1754–88. Here Cardinal Richelieu, Molière and Madame de Pompadour were baptised; Louis XIV made his first holy communion; Lully was married; and Louis XIV's minister, Colbert, La Fontaine, Molière and Mirabeau had their funerals. St-Eustache also saw the premieres of Berlioz' *Te Deum* and Liszt's *Messe de Gran*.

To the east, the small **Square des Innocents** began life as a graveyard, enclosed in 1186. It is said that during the siege of 1590 food in Paris became so short that locals ground bones from the charnel-house for flour. In 1780 an estimated two million corpses were finally removed to the Catacombs (see page 94). Today, the square contains several fast-food joints, numerous buskers and the enchanting Renaissance **Fontaine des Innocents**, designed by Pierre Lescot and carved by Jean Goujon in 1548, and moved here in 1788.

BEAUBOURG ★★★
(metro: Hotel de Ville/Châtelet-Les Halles)
In the 1960s the poverty-stricken and ironically named Beaubourg (beautiful town) was cleared. In its place, from 1972–7, President Georges Pompidou commissioned two architects, British Richard Rogers and Italian Renzo Piano, to create a globally renowned centre for the arts. The controversial, futuristic, inside-out **Centre Georges Pompidou**, *19 rue Beaubourg, 4th,* fostered a whole new wave of modern design.

MULTI-COLOURED SCAFFOLDING

The structure of the Pompidou Centre is made of fourteen 12.8m (43ft) porticoes, each with two steel pillars 50m (165ft) apart. These are filled with water for added weight and fire protection. Each of the five floors is a vast open space of 7500m² (80,000 sq ft) (the size of two football pitches). The technical shafts are all on the outside of the building. Those painted blue are for air-conditioning, green are for fluids (eg water), yellow are for electrical shafts and red are for communication (eg lifts and escalators). The vast white pipes on the roof are the air-cooling ducts.

Take the glassed-in escalator up to the 5th floor and work down. As you rise the view expands outwards, while at your feet people swarm in ever-changing patterns around the many buskers in the piazza. The 5th floor is used for major international exhibitions.

The superb permanent collection of the **Musée National d'Art Moderne** covers work from the beginning of the 20th century to the present day. The so-called 'historic' collection (1905–65) is on the 4th floor, arranged chronologically but with the greatest works, by artists such as Matisse, Picasso, Kandinsky and Léger, easily

The innovative Georges Pompidou Centre has become a major cultural magnet with numerous exhibition areas as well as media resources of all kinds.

Le Défenseur du Temps in the Quartier de l'Horloge hourly fights the age-old battle against time and the elements.

accessible in the main gallery. Side galleries are devoted to individual artists or movements. On the 3rd floor the gallery comes bang up to date, with continually changing exhibitions on current trends and new artists.

Other facilities include the Centre de Création Industrielle, devoted to industrial and commercial design; IRCAM (the Institute of Sound and Music Research and Coordination); public libraries; and performance spaces with regular lectures, live performances and films.

The south wall abuts **Place Igor Stravinsky**, where Niki de Saint-Phalle's brightly coloured water sculptures, dedicated to works by Stravinsky, create an atmosphere of perpetual carnival. Between are black metal mobiles by Jean Tinguely. Narrow Rue St Martin leads south past the flamboyant Gothic **Eglise de St-Merri** (1520–1612), formerly parish church of the moneylenders in the Rue des Lombards. Look for the small hermaphroditic demon above the door. The interior was heavily altered during the reign of Louis XV.

To the north of the Pompidou Centre, in the **Quartier de l'Horloge**, is Jacques Monastier's **Le Défenseur du Temps**, *rue Bernard-de-Clairvaux, 3rd*, a magnificent 4m (13ft) high public clock of polished brass. On the hour, the warrior has to fend off the earth (dragon), the air (eagle) or the sea (crab), complete with thundering sound effects. At 12:00 and 18:00 he manages to defeat all the creatures as they assault him together.

The nearby **Musée des Instruments Musicales Mécaniques**, *Impasse Berthaud, 3rd*, is an enchanting, family-run collection of working hurdy-gurdies, music boxes and barrel organs dating back to the 18th century.

THE MARAIS ★★★
(metro: Saint-Paul/Chemin Vert)

The name 'Marais' means 'marsh' and until the 16th century no scheme to drain and develop the unhealthy swamp really succeeded. The Templars tried, but their 13th-century walled town did not survive the disbanding of the order in 1307. Philippe-Auguste included the district in his walled city and in 1358, after the mob invaded the Conciergerie, the future Charles V lived for a while in the now defunct Hôtel St Pol.

The place only really began to take off in the 17th century when Henry IV built the **Place des Vosges** in 1605. Known originally as the Place Royale, it was renamed by Napoleon after the first département in France to pay its taxes! This elegantly restrained and beautiful square is one of the few true Renaissance structures in Paris. Nine identical brick fronted houses line each side, broken only by the porticoed pavilions of the King and Queen (Henry and his wife lived separate lives). Underneath is a colonnade which now shelters a wealth of small antique shops and restaurants. The open square was popular for promenading and duels until the

HENRI IV

Born in 1553, son of the Duc de Vendôme and the Queen of Navarre, Henri began his political life as commander-in-chief of the Huguenot forces during the Wars of Religion. His marriage to Marguerite de Valois in 1572, sister of Charles IX, meant to symbolise the peace treaty, was in fact used to spark the horrendous St Bartholomew's Day Massacre, organised by his mother-in-law, Cathérine de Medici. In 1593, Henri converted to Catholicism in order to inherit the crown of France, supposedly saying "Paris is worth a mass." His heart always remained Protestant, however, and, in 1598, he signed the Edict of Nantes, guaranteeing freedom of worship.

He married a second time in 1600, to Marie de Medici. It was an unhappy liaison and though they did manage to produce a son and heir, Louis XIII, they lived separate lives, both indulging in numerous affairs. Henri was assassinated in 1610 by a fanatical Jesuit. He is still remembered fondly as one of the greatest, most liberal and most efficient of French kings.

An equestrian statue of Louis XIII surveys the elegant and architecturally consistent Place des Vosges laid out by Henri IV.

This bakery caters for the Jewish community that has been established in Paris for 700 years.

MARAIS WALK

Start at metro St Paul. Go right along Rue St Antoine, past the Church of St Louis-St Paul and the Hotel de Sully. Turn left up Rue de Birague into Place des Vosges. At the top of the square, turn left into Rue des Francs Bourgeois, right into Rue Sévigné, past the Musée Carnavalet and left into Rue du Parc Royal. To the right, on Rue Thorigny, is the Musée Picasso. Go straight on. The road becomes Rue des 4 Fils. Turn left into Rue des Archives and left again, back onto Rue des Francs Bourgeois. Turn right on Rue Pavée and you will come out on Rue St Antoine, near the metro station.

garden was created in 1685. Richelieu lived at no 21; at no 6 you can visit a small museum dedicated to Victor Hugo, who lived here from 1832–48.

Around this stately square sprang up a new district as the rich and titled scrambled for a place in the heart of fashion. The result is a harmonious maze of small streets and squares, complete with some 100 surviving 17th- and 18th-century mansions. Although the area became very run down, it miraculously survived the post-war bulldozers and is today a conservation area of enormous charm and character.

The **Musée Carnavalet**, *23 rue de Sévigné, 3rd*, is housed in the Hôtel Carnavalet, built in 1548, but heavily altered by Mansart in 1655–60. In the courtyard is a magnificent statue of Louis XIV by Coysevox. The museum is dedicated to the history of Paris as told through art. In theory, it runs in chronological order, but it is a total maze and virtually impossible to navigate successfully. Exhibits include several complete rooms, among them the suite of a former owner, 18th-century society hostess and renowned letter writer, Madame de Sévigné; Marcel Proust's bedroom; the art nouveau Fouquet Jewellery Boutique; and the 1924 ballroom of the Hôtel Wendel, painted by José-María Sert. Look also for the detailed model of Paris in 1527, a model of the Bastille carved from one of its stones (a popular and lucrative souvenir), a toy guillotine, and the roomful of shop signs. Above all, there are paintings documenting almost every important person and event in the history of the city.

The **Musée Picasso**, *5 rue de Thorigny, 3rd*, lives in the Hôtel Salé, built in 1656 by Jean Boullier, who made his fortune in salt tax. Inside is a superb collection of work by the late, great Pablo (1881–1973), donated to the state in lieu of inheritance tax. There are few major works, but every period is represented in 200 paintings, 3000 drawings and engravings, and every medium from ceramics to illustrated manuscripts. A sculpture garden, an audio-visual room and a gallery dedicated to Picasso's own collection, with works by Braque, Cézanne, Matisse and Rousseau, completes the exhibition.

Ernest Cognac, wealthy founder of La Samaritaine (see page 39) and his wife, Louise Jay, were passionate devotees of the 18th century. Their private collection forms the core of the delightful **Musée Cognacq-Jay**, *Hôtel Donon, 8 rue Elzévir, 3rd*, dedicated to a period of charming froth. Works by Canaletto, Fragonard and Boucher add weight.

There are several other small museums in the area, all in palatial houses whose architecture alone is worth a look. The **Musée Kwok-On**, *41 rue des Francs Bourgeois, 4th*, has a fascinating collection on oriental theatre and street festivals, complete with puppets, costumes and masks. The **Musée National des Techniques**, in the former priory of St-Martin-des-Champs, *292 rue St Martin, 3rd (metro: Arts et Métiers, Strasbourg St Denis)*, traces the development of science and technology from the 16th to the 20th century. The documentary **Musée Historique de France** offers the only public access to the National Archives and two of the most magnificent buildings in the Marais, the Hôtel de Soubise (1554 and rebuilt in 1705), *60 rue des Francs-Bourgeois, 4th*, and the Hôtel de Rohan (1705), *87 rue Vieille du Temple, 4th*. The **Musée de la Chasse et de Nature**, Hôtel Guénégaud (*c*1650), *60 rue des Archives, 3rd*, has dead animals and paintings of hunting. The **Musée de la Serrure**, Hôtel Libéral Bruant (1685), *1 rue de la Perle, 3rd*, has a collection of locks, from the Roman era onwards. The **Bibliothèque Historique de la Ville de Paris** is in the Hôtel Lamoignan (1518 and 1718), *24 rue Pavée, 4th*. The **Pavillon de l'Arsénal** (1564), *1 rue de Sully, 4th*, has an exhibition about the history, and future architectural planning, of Paris.

Finally, take a look at two other houses, the brick-patterned **Maison de Jacques Coeur** (*c*1440), *rue des*

DEATHLY PROTEST

In 1627, Cardinal Richelieu banned duelling. On 12 May, a group of six hot-headed noblemen gathered in front of his windows at 21 Place des Vosges, to fight a duel in protest. The Comte de Montmorency, La Berthe and des Chapelles took on the Marquise de Beuvron, Bussy d'Amboise and Buquet. Bussy was killed, La Berthe was wounded and Beuvron and Buquet escaped to England. Montmorency and des Chapelles were not so lucky. Arrested and condemned to death, they were beheaded in the Grève (place de l'Hôtel de Ville).

Archives, 4th, built by Charles VII's financial adviser, and one of the oldest houses in Paris. Framed for poisoning the king's mistress, Coeur was stripped of all lands and money. His innocence was acknowledged a year after his death in exile in 1457. The **Hôtel de Beauvais** (1657), *68 rue François-Miron, 4th*, was built by Catherine Belliers, a maid ennobled by Marie de Medici for her ability to give a good enema and for assuring the queen, from first-hand experience, of her son's sexual prowess! Other particularly fine houses include: **Hôtel des Ambassadeurs de Hollande** (1655; also known as Amelot de Bisseuil), *47 rue Vieille du Temple, 3rd*; **Hôtel d'Aumont** (1645), *7 rue de Jouy, 4th*; **Maison de Jean Hérouët** (1510), *42 rue des Francs-Bourgeois, 4th*; and **Hôtel de Sens** (1475-1507), *1 rue du Figuier, 4th*.

Since the 13th century the Marais has also been home to the Jewish community in Paris, centred on the **Rue des Rosiers**. A new wave of settlement by Sephardic Jews from North Africa revived the area after World War II and you will find several working synagogues and Jewish restaurants in the area. The **Mémorial du Martyr Juif Inconnu**, *17 rue Geoffroy-l'Asnier, 4th*, has a small museum about the Jewish struggle against Nazism and an eternal flame for victims of the Holocaust.

Rue St Antoine, the widest street in the district, is an extension of the Rue de Rivoli, based on a Roman road. In 1559 Montgomery, the Scottish captain of the guards, fatally wounded Henry II during a tournament here to celebrate the marriage

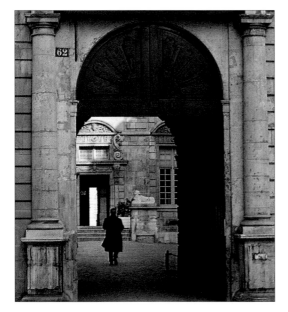

The archway to the Hôtel de Sully. The façade of the building has been restored to its original 17th-century appearance.

The fortress-like Opéra Bastille, built to commemorate the storming of the Bastille prison in 1789, adds a further dimension to the city's cultural facilities.

St Gervais St Protais

At the corner of the Rue François-Miron, following the route of the old Roman road from Paris to Senlis, is the church of St Gervais and St Protais. Dedicated to two Roman martyrs, the church was founded in the 6th century, but the present building dates from the 16th. Its façade displays all three orders of classical architecture – Doric, Ionic and Corinthian – while the interior is Gothic with interesting decorative details. The church is most known for its connections with music, and several members of the Couperin family were employed there as organists over a period of 170 years, among them composer François Couperin (1668–1733). Place St Gervais is also noteworthy for its elm tree, under which judicicial decisions were made in the Middle Ages.

of Henry's daughter to Phillip II of Spain. Montgomery fled, and the king died ten days later in the Hôtel de Tournelles. His widow, Cathérine de Medici, tore down the building and, 15 years later, captured and executed Montgomery, as soon as he set foot on French soil. The **Eglise de St-Louis-St-Paul** was built by the Jesuits in 1641. Once equally luxuriant inside and out, it lost its fine furnishings during the Revolution and seems spartan these days. The beautiful **Hôtel de Sully** (1625), no 62, now houses the Caisse Nationale des Monuments Historiques et des Sites, and has a superb bookshop that specializes in all things Parisian.

BASTILLE

Not a trace remains of the Bastille, except an outline in the paving stones of the **Place de la Bastille** *(metro: Bastille)* and a short stretch of the foundations, seen from the metro platform (Line 5). Built in 1367–82 to guard the eastern Porte St Antoine against the British, the fortress expanded into a huge castle with eight towers. In spite of this, it was captured six times in seven sieges. As a prison, it was used mainly to lock up those who offended the king and nothing like as grim as the Conciergerie and Châtelet. Many of the wealthy inmates had comfortably furnished rooms, good meals and their own servants. Ironically, the government gave the order to demolish the prison two weeks before the crowd did it for them on 14 July 1789, a date which is celebrated annually by the French. When the 600-strong mob arrived, they found only seven prisoners left to free – and only one of them was a political detainee. Citizen Palloy, who took charge of the demolition, made a fortune selling the stones for building or carving them into models of the Bastille as souvenirs. The key to the Bastille was given to US President George Washington.

Napoleon's plans to erect a 6m (20ft) bronze elephant in the newly formed square came to nothing and its plinth was used to erect the **Colonne de Juillet 1830**, as a memorial to those who died in the three-day 1830 revolution. The winged figure on top, also on the 10F piece, represents the Genius of Liberty.

The cool, crisp **Opéra Bastille**, designed by Carlos Ott, a Canadian-Uruguayan architect, was opened in 1989 to celebrate the Bicentennial of the Revolution. It is suffering a little financially, but has begun to resurrect a run-down area. The existing Opéra was renamed Opéra Garnier (see page 67) to avoid confusion.

Opposite: *The infamous Bastille prison is now only a tracing in the pavement. In its place stand the 1830 July Column and the Opéra Bastille, built in 1989.*

The Cimetière de Père Lachaise ★★

(metro: Père Lachaise, Philippe-Auguste)

Named after Louis XIV's confessor and founded in 1804, this has become the largest and most interesting of the great Parisian cemeteries, with a starry list of inhabitants, many of whom were moved from elsewhere to help popularize it. Many of its tombs are impressive monuments and the cemetery is visited as much for its sculptural contents as for its occupants. A map of celebrity graves is available at the gate. Writers include Fontaine, Molière, Beaumarchais, Colette, Proust, Balzac, Hugo, Oscar Wilde and Gertrude Stein. Musicians include Chopin, Fauré, Rossini, Bizet, Edith Piaf, Jim Morrison (of The Doors). Art lovers should look for Corot, Bellini, David, Modigliani and Delacroix, and theatregoers for Sarah Bernhardt, Simone Signoret and Isadora Duncan. Other notables include Baron Haussmann, Marshal Ney and Abélard and Héloïse.

The Paris Commune made its last stand here on 28 May 1871. Many died during the fighting and the last 147 alive were shot against the Mur des Fédérés, in the south-east corner. They are buried where they fell, in a communal grave where flowers are still left.

There is also a memorial to the many French who died in Nazi concentration camps or as a result of their work with the French Resistance during World War II.

ABELARD AND HELOISE

Brilliant 12th-century philosopher, Peter Abélard (1079–1142) fell passionately in love with his pupil, Héloïse, the beautiful young niece of his landlord, Canon Filbert. She refused to marry him, and when she eventually became pregnant, Abélard packed her off to a convent, where she lived to a ripe old age and became abbess. Her enraged uncle had Abélard castrated. He retaliated; the Canon lost his home, position and wealth, after which Abélard retired to a monastery in St Denis. The couple never met again while alive, but are buried together in Père Lachaise Cemetery.

4
Montmartre and the North-East

MONTMARTRE ***

(metro: Anvers – for the funicular, Abbesses, Lamarck-Caulaincourt)

A centre of pre-historic sun worship, dedicated to Mercury by the Romans, 129m (423 ft) high Montmartre was renamed in the 9th century after St Denis, martyred here in AD262 (see page 99). It is the highest point in Paris, known to locals simply as 'la butte' (the hill). There is an excellent view from the steps of the basilica.

Until Haussmann enclosed it within the city walls in 1860, Montmartre remained a small, relatively peaceful village. Henry IV brought canons up here during his siege, and Cossacks occupied the area after Napoleon's downfall in 1814. In 1871, however, the National Guard holed up here and declared the Paris Commune (see page 14), an action which led to 20,000 deaths and the near destruction of Paris.

Meanwhile, in 1673–89, a local nun had several visions of Christ, who asked for a church of the Sacred Heart. During the dark days of the Franco-Prussian War (1870), two businessmen vowed to build it if France were spared; the church was eventually completed in 1910 and consecrated in 1919. The huge sugary-white dome of the **Basilique du Sacré Coeur** now dominates the skyline of Paris. The fanciful architect, Paul Abadie, who delighted in sticking Byzantine domes on everything he built, let his imagination run riot, creating a magnificent pastiche that has most architectural critics foaming at the mouth, but is adored by those who appreciate late Victorian

MONTMARTRE WALK

Start at the top of the funicular. Visit the Basilica, then walk down past St Pierre, turn left, then right into Rue du Mont Cenis. Take the first left, then right into Rue des Saules. Follow this down the hill to the Musée d'Art Juif. Retrace your steps to the top, into the Place du Tertre. From here, head downhill on Rue Lépic. Near the bottom, it becomes Rue des Abbesses, leading into Place des Abbesses, where you will find a metro stop.

Opposite: *The glistening basilica of Sacré Coeur was built by the nation as a mark of repentance and devotion after the Franco-Prussian War.*

architecture. Inside, Luc Olivier Merson's vast mosaic of Christ swoops over the high altar, arms akimbo, the heroes of France at his feet. Since 1 August 1885, without exception, a rota of locals have prayed here every hour for the sins of the Commune to be forgiven.

Founded by Louis VI and Queen Adelaide of Savoy (who later became the first abbess) in 1133 as part of a once-powerful convent, the **Eglise de St-Pierre-de-Montmartre**, *place St Pierre, 18th*, is totally dwarfed. It has some fine Romanesque capitals, an 18th-century façade, and 20th-century stained glass.

But to most people, Montmartre is all about its glory years as the focus of the artistic world. The artists began to arrive in about 1840, drawn in by the paintable surroundings, golden light and cheap rents. They lived mainly on the breadline – Puccini based his tragic opera *La Bohème* on their uncomfortable existence – yet they tapped a well of genius and created a legend that draws millions to Paris each year. By about 1920 rents had risen and the artists moved to Montparnasse.

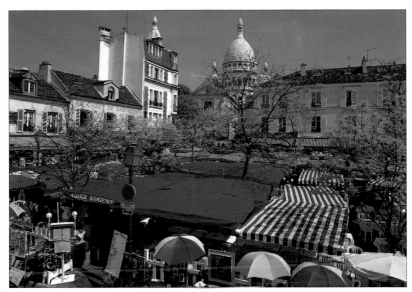

The focus of the 'village', the pretty **Place du Tertre**, is now a heaving mass of pavement artists (licensed at two easels per square metre) and gawping tourists. It is still fun to look and the atmosphere bubbles, but most of the art is sadly third-rate while the many cafés and restaurants are grossly overpriced. **La Mère Cathérine**, founded in 1793, is said to have been where the term 'bistro' originated, coined by Cossack forces in search of quick service (see page 28). Nearby, the cavernous **Espace Montmartre Salvador Dali**, *rue Poulbot, 18th*, has a beautifully displayed collection of 330 paintings, drawings and sculptures by the master surrealist.

Several of the greatest local artists, including Renoir, Van Gogh, Dufy, Suzanne Valadon and Utrillo, all lived at *12 rue Cortot, 18th*. Today, it is home to the **Musée du Vieux Montmartre**, dedicated to the history and artistic life of the hill, with old photos, maps and plans, posters by Toulouse-Lautrec and other Bohemian memorabilia.

Beyond this, the deceptively rustic **Lapin Agile**, *22 rue des Saules, 18th*, is a famous cabaret, home to some of the most biting satirical comedy in Paris. It gained its

The brightly canopied cafés of the Place du Tertre just round the corner from the Sacré Coeur provide an ideal setting for artists keen to sell souvenir paintings of Montmartre.

DON'T MISS

*** **Sacré Coeur**: overblown and fantastic, this church is a glorious folly, with superb views
*** **The streets and cafés of Montmartre**
*** **The Cité des Sciences**: Paris' homage to science and technology.

name from the delightful sign of an escaping rabbit, painted by André Gil (le lapin à Gil). A little further on, the last **vineyard** in Paris was replanted in 1886. The grapes are harvested amidst great festivities on the first Saturday in October each year and crushed for a very indifferent gamay, *Clos de Montmartre*, sold in aid of the local old people. At *no 42, rue des Saules, 18th*, the **Musée d'Art Juif** is dedicated to religious and secular Jewish art, from across the centuries and the globe. Highlights include model synagogues from Lithuania and Poland and an illustrated Bible by Marc Chagall.

Rue Lépic is the longest and most gentle route up the hill. At no 77, the much-painted **Moulin de la Gallette** (1622), is one of two surviving windmills (out of an origi-

nal 30). In 1814 the Cossacks crucified the miller on one of the sails, after which the family decided to give up on flour. Further down the road, there is a good market.

Pigalle is best known for its nightlife, centred on the famous **Moulin Rouge**, *82 boulevard de Clichy, 18th*, which opened in 1885 and is still going strong. The side streets support a bevy of prostitutes and clubs to cater for all tastes. Single women should avoid the area after dark. The turquoise tile and brick-clad church of **St Jean l'Evangéliste**, *Place des Abbesses, 18th*, was designed by Anatole de Baudot (1904), the first church in France to be built in concrete. The **Chapelle du Martyre**, *9 rue Yvonne-le-Tac, 18th*, is the latest 19th-century chapel on

Left: *The Moulin Rouge has been famous for its Parisian nightlife since the 1890s and was painted by the artist Toulouse-Lautrec.*

Opposite, top: *Painted café sign.*

Opposite, bottom: *The quaint charm of Le Lapin Agile belies its reputation as a hotbed of satire.*

the spot where St Denis was martyred. In 1534 St Ignatius Loyola and his followers gathered in the crypt to found the Society of Jesus (the Jesuits). The delightful **Musée d'Art Naïf Max Fournay**, Halle-St-Pierre, *2 rue Ronsard, 18th*, has a cheerful, unusual collection of naive art and children's exhibitions and workshops.

The **Cimetière de Montmartre**, *20 av Rachel, 18th (metro: place de Clichy)*, is one of the great, romantic Parisian cemeteries founded in the early 19th century. Inhabitants include Stendhal, Zola, Dumas the younger, Fragonard, Berlioz, Degas, Nijinsky, Delibes, Offenbach, François Truffaut and Alphonsine Plessis, immortalized as *La Traviata* and *La Dame aux Camélias*.

Other museums in the area include **Musée Edith Piaf**, *5 rue Crespin-du-Gast, 11th (metro: Ménilmontant)*. A superb singer, the 'little sparrow' (1915–63) was born on a street corner but went on to become the toast of the world. Open by appointment; tel: 43 55 52 72. The **Musée de la Vie Romantique**, *16 rue Chaptal, 9th (metro: St Georges, Blanche)*, has memoirs of George Sand, and her family and inner circle in a typically bourgeois 19th-century home. The **Musée de Cristal de Baccarat**, *30bis rue Paradis, 10th (metro: Gare de l'Est)*, is the glittering show-piece of the crystal factory founded in 1764.

In 1860 Haussmann turned a deserted quarry and rubbish dump into the delightful **Parc des Buttes-Chaumont**, *rue Manin, 19th (metro: Botzaris, Buttes-Chaumont)*, with tumbling water, cliffs and lavish greenery.

STREET ARCHITECTURE

The Place des Abbesses is a good monument to two of the least known artistic patrons of Paris. The splendid, swirling metro entrance is a rare surviving example of the original design by Art Nouveau architect, Hector Guimard (1867–1942). The small, green drinking fountain is one of many donated to Paris by the 19th-century English philanthropist, Sir Richard Wallace (1818–90), who also ran two field hospitals and several feeding stations during the 1870 siege. His private art collection is now on display in London.

The Bassin de la Villette is a dock for the Parisian network of canals, and is in turn linked to the Seine by the Canal St Martin.

Parc de La Villette ***

30 av. Corentin-Cariou, 19th (metro: Porte de la Villette)
For over a century this seedy quarter was home to the Paris stockyards, a chaos of live animals, abattoirs and butchers. In the 1960s refrigeration came in and the whole web collapsed, leaving the world's largest slaughter-house empty. In 1986 a 55ha (136 acre) showcase complex rose like a phoenix, with the aid of architect Adrian Fainsilber, to become one of the top attractions in Paris.

To get there the most enjoyable way, take a boat trip along the pretty **Canal St Martin**, which connects the Seine with the **Bassin de la Villette**, and beyond that, the Canal de l'Ourcq (see page 120). It was built in 1825 for handling freight; for 2km (1¹/₄ miles) it runs underground. The charming round **Rotonde de la Villette** (1784) was built as a customs house.

The slaughterhouse itself has become the super high-tech **Cité des Sciences et de l'Industrie**, a sparkling inter-active hands-on museum designed to keep all ages and people, including the most technically inept, enthralled for hours. The main body is known as the **Explora**, with three vast floors dedicated to permanent exhibitions on Space, the Ocean, the Environment, Cultivating Land, Bio-technology, Language and Communication, Mathematics, Sound, Light, Energy, Health and the Human Body, Computer Technology, the Earth, Sea and Stars. A high-tech soil-free greenhouse and a supersonic bomber are suspended in the rafters and there is a special Cité des Enfants for 3–12 year olds, with plenty for them to do.

Inside the Explora are also a **Planetarium** and the 3D **Cinéma Louis-Lumière**. Outside, the **Géode** is a massive geodesic sphere made of 6500 stainless steel triangles, with a 1000m² (10,750 sq ft) hemispherical cinema screen. The even more unsettling **Cinaxe** moves and shakes the entire cinema as you watch. The **Cité de la Musique** has music and dance schools, workshop and performance spaces and a music museum. There is also a theatre, and the Grande Halle is used for jazz.

The gigantic Géode screen at the Cité des Sciences et de l'Industrie invites the visitor to glimpse a futuristic world.

Other attractions include the park itself, with playgrounds and sculptures, follies, an **Aquarium** and even an example of a 1957 submarine, **L'Argonaut**. The **Zénith** is a huge polyester tent that holds 6000, designed as a concert venue.

5
The Louvre and Opéra

THE LOUVRE ***
(metro: Louvre-Rivoli, Palais-Royal)
The Louvre is not only one of the greatest art galleries,
but also the largest royal palace in the world. Allow
plenty of time, wear comfortable shoes and don't even
try to see everything. It is a sightseeing marathon with
32 km (18 miles) of corridors.

The first fortress was built here by Philippe-Auguste
in 1200, since when numerous monarchs have extended
the vast, lavish patchwork of palatial apartments and
courtyards. Around the central Cour Napoléon are the
northern Richelieu Wing, the southern section of the
palace, the Denon Wing, and the eastern Sully Wing
which leads through to the Cour Carrée and Claude
Perrault's 17th-century colonnade. An excavated area
shows the remnants of the early fortress. To the right are
the Jardin du Carrousel and Jardin des Tuileries.

The ultra-modern glass pyramid was added in 1988
by architect I. M. Pei, as the new main entrance to the
museum. From the Halle Napoléon separate escalators
lead to the three wings. A free colour-coded plan is available to help you find your personal highlights. Blue is for
ground floor; red for first floor; and yellow, second floor.
The prize exhibits are always surrounded by vast
crowds; elsewhere there are equally stunning works of
art with half the number of people.

Most famous of all is the *Mona Lisa* (*La Joconde* in
French), brought to the city by Leonardo da Vinci himself, during the reign of François I, who started the col-

LE GRANDE AXE HISTORIQUE

This triumphant way sweeping through the heart of Paris
was laid out by the 17th-
century landscape gardener,
Le Nôtre. It starts in the
courtyard of the Louvre with
the Arc du Carrousel (25m
[82ft]), runs across the Place
de la Concorde and up the
Champs-Elysées to the Arc de
Triomphe (50m [164ft]) and
culminates in the Grande
Arche de la Défense (100m
[328ft]). The length is about
8km (5 miles); both the
courtyard of the Louvre and
the Grand Arche are angled
at 6° 33' from the exact line
of the Axe.

Opposite: *I. M. Pei's
glass pyramid is the latest
contribution to the much-
rebuilt Louvre.*

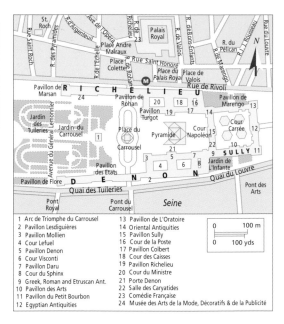

1 Arc de Triomphe du Carrousel	13 Pavillon de L'Oratoire
2 Pavillon Lesdiguières	14 Oriental Antiquities
3 Pavillon Mollien	15 Pavillon Sully
4 Cour Lefuel	16 Cour de la Poste
5 Pavillon Denon	17 Pavillon Colbert
6 Cour Visconti	18 Cour des Caisses
7 Pavillon Daru	19 Pavillon Richelieu
8 Cour du Sphinx	20 Cour du Ministre
9 Greek, Roman and Etruscan Ant.	21 Porte Denon
10 Pavillon des Arts	22 Salle des Caryatides
11 Pavillon du Petit Bourbon	23 Comédie Française
12 Egyptian Antiquities	24 Musée des Arts de la Mode, Décoratifs & de la Publicité

Boats for hire to sail on the Octagonal Basin in the Jardins des Tuileries.

lection with twelve paintings by the masters of the day. His royal successors and many of their ministers were also avid collectors and by the time the museum opened in 1793 it was already one of the richest bodies of art in the world. Almost every great European artist is represented here. Amongst the paintings, also look out for the satirical *Ship of Fools* (Hieronymus Bosch); Leonardo's exquisite *Virgin with the Infant Jesus and St Anne* and *Virgin of the Rocks*; Botticelli's *Venus and the Graces*; and Vermeer's *Lacemaker*. The finer scupltures include the *Marly Horses* (Guillaume Costou) which originally graced the Place de la Concorde, and Michelangelo's *Slaves*.

The 2nd-century BC *Venus de Milo*, bought from the Greeks in 1820, is the highlight of the vast Ancient collection, which covers the Roman, Greek, Etruscan, Egyptian and several Middle Eastern civilizations. Other highlights include the vast granite *Sphinx* and *Squatting Scribe* (both 4th dynasty, *c*2500BC), and the Greek *Winged Victory of Samothrace*.

The Pope Being Shown Building Plans *on view in the Louvre.*

The biggest draw amongst the objets d'art is usually the 140-carat *Regent Diamond* amongst the Crown Jewels.

Also in the palace are the **Musée des Arts de la Mode**, *109 rue de Rivoli, 1st*, dedicated to the history of fashion with a gorgeous collection of haute couture and historical costumes, and the **Musée des Arts Décoratifs**, *107 rue de Rivoli, 1st*, dedicated to decorative and ornamental art, furniture and furnishings from the Middle Ages to the present day. Look out for the art nouveau and art deco rooms, the collection of 60,000 posters and the dolls *(metro for both: Palais-Royal, Tuileries)*.

The **Arc de Triomphe du Carrousel**, built by Napoleon to mark his 1805 victories, is closely modelled on the Roman Arch of Septimius Severus. It was originally topped by the four famous horses of St Mark's, Venice; they were returned in 1815 along with all the other artistic treasures Napoleon had looted from around Europe. Beyond this stretch the **Jardins des Tuileries**. In 1560 Cathérine de Medici bought a derelict tile works *(tuileries)* and laid out the first gardens. They were redesigned by Le Nôtre in 1664 and still follow his formal plan, with small, forbidden lawns, serried rows of identical plants and wide walkways lined by uncomfortable benches. There are several fine statues, including

---

TIMETABLE OF THE LOUVRE

1200 Philippe-Auguste builds first fortress

1360s Charles V converts it to a royal residence.

1527–46 François I starts remodelling to convert it to a Renaissance palace. Work, overseen by Lescot, with sculpture by Jean Goujon, continues through the reigns of Henry II, Charles IX and Henry III.

1563 Cathérine de Medici commissions Philippe Delorme to build the Palais des Tuileries and Waterside Gallery. Work continues through until Henry IV's death in 1610.

1627 Louis XIII builds the Pavillon de l'Horloge.

1659–70 Louis XIV builds the Cour Carrée and extends the Tuileries.

1805–15 Napoleon extends the northern arm to the Pavillon de Marsan.

1852–70 Napoleon III builds new pavilions around the Cour Napoléon.

1988–9 I. M. Pei adds glass pyramid.

four by Rodin, but the one real point of gaiety is the Octagonal Basin, a large pond surrounded by a phalanx of ice-cream sellers, where generations of children have sailed their colourful toy boats.

At the far end is the enchanting **Orangerie**, *place de la Concorde, 1st (metro: Concorde),* home to an excellent small collection, including works by Cézanne, Matisse, Renoir, Utrillo, Douanier Rousseau and Modigliani. At its heart is a place of almost magical serenity designed to house, in perfect surroundings, eight of Monet's vast, almost abstract waterlily paintings, each showing a different impression of light and atmosphere. Next door, the **Jeu**

The Palais Royal was rebuilt in the 18th century by Duke Philippe II, but it was his grandson Louis-Philippe who enclosed the gardens on three sides with arcades of shops in order to provide an income.

de Paume, *20 rue Royale, 1st (metro: Concorde, Tuileries)*, is a former 'real tennis' court which hosts regular temporary exhibitions of modern art.

The **Palais Royal** *(metro: Palais Royal)* was built in 1624 for Cardinal Richelieu. He left it to Louis XIV (in case he was short of palaces), who handed it on to his brother, Philippe d'Orléans. The palace is closed to the public, but the delightful colonnaded Cour d'Honneur and gardens are accessible. In 1781 Philippe sold off building lots around the gardens, creating an enclosed, highly popular centre of drinking, gambling and prostitution (now all gone). The steel balls in the fountains and the black and white pillars in the court were added in 1986 by Daniel Buren.

To one side of the main entrance, the 1786 **Théâtre Français**, *2 rue de Richelieu, 1st*, is still home to the country's most prestigious theatre company, the Comédie Française (see page 21). In the foyer is the chair in which Molière died in 1673, on stage during a performance of *Le Malade Imaginaire*. Behind the palace is the **Bibliothèque Nationale**, *52 rue de Richelieu, 1st (metro: Bourse)*. This priceless library has been in existence since 1370; since 1537 any book published in France has been added by law. The collection, which is one of the largest in Europe, now holds over 12 million publications. The library is due to move out to new purpose-built premises. Inside, as well as books and great architecture, is a glorious little

WALK

Start at metro Palais-Royal and walk west along Rue de Rivoli. Turn right into Rue Castiglione, cross Place Vendôme and continue up Rue de la Paix to the Place de l'Opéra. Turn left along Boulevard des Capucines, which turns into Boulevard de la Madeleine, coming out beside the Eglise de la Madeleine (see page 71). Walk down into Place de la Concorde, turn into the Tuileries Gardens and follow them back to the Louvre courtyard, and from there back to the metro.

*Paris' numerous cafés,
parks and gardens provide
a tranquil haven in a
bustling city.*

**A SCULPTURE FOR ALL
SEASONS**

The first sculpture in the
Place Vendôme was an
equestrian Louis XIV as a
Roman emperor. Napoleon I
put up the Vendôme Column
topped by a statue of himself
as Julius Caesar. The
Bourbons melted this down
and used the metal for a new
statue of Henry IV, moved to
the Pont Neuf in 1815. Louis
XVIII put up a Bourbon fleur-
de-lis; Louis-Philippe took it
down and put up another
statue of his uncle, in military
uniform. Napoleon III sent
that to Les Invalides and put
up yet another statue of
Napoleon I, as a Roman. The
entire column was demol-
ished by Communards in
1871 and replaced by a copy,
including the original Roman
Napoleon, under the Third
Republic.

---

museum, the **Cabinet des Médailles et des Antiques**,
containing the treasure-trove of the kings of France, St-
Denis and the Sainte-Chapelle. Lovers of expensive
baubles and things that gleam will be in their element.
Nearby are also several charming arcades, including the
Galerie Véro-Dodat, Galerie Colbert and Galerie Vivienne.

The **Eglise de St Roch** (patron saint of plague victims), *rue St-Honoré, 1st (metro: Tuileries)*, was built in
1653–1730. Regular outbreaks of plague stopped at about
the same time. The bullet holes in the façade were added
on 5 October 1795, when Napoleon led an artillery troop
against a royalist uprising. As a reward, he was given
command of the French troops in Italy. Inside are several
fine paintings and the tombs of Le Nôtre and Corneille.

As well as all his other building work, Louis XIV felt
he needed to add two new royal squares to Paris. The
larger **Place Vendôme**, built in 1702–20 by Hardouin-
Mansart, is a gracious classical octagon surrounded by an
arcade and named after the Hôtel Vendôme which had
previously occupied the site. Napoleon erected the
Vendôme Column to commemorate his victory at
Austerlitz in 1805. A replica of Trajan's Column in Rome,
it stands 44m (144ft) high, has a stone core around which
is a spiral of bronze reliefs, cast from 1250 cannons captured during the battle. The whole column is a copy of
the original, destroyed in 1871. The harmony of the **Place
des Victoires**, a little further east, has been damaged by
the ravages of time and revolution. Just north of this, the
neo-classical **Bourse**, *place de la Bourse, 2nd (metro: Bourse)*,
was designed by Alexandre-Théodore Brongniart. It has
been the home of the Paris Stock Exchange since 1808.

OPERA

In 1660–1705 Louis XIV knocked down the city wall,
filled in the moat and created the Boulevard. From about
1750 the road became a fashionable promenade. In 1860
Haussmann got to work, carving out a series of **Grands
Boulevards** – Capucines, Italiens, Haussmann,
Montmartre, Poissonnière, Bonne Nouvelle, Saint-Denis,
Saint-Martin, Temple, Filles de Calvaire and

Beaumarchais. Together, they now make up a heaving shopping centre, the Parisian equivalent of Oxford Street. Pride of place goes to three department stores, Galeries Lafayette, au Printemps – and Marks and Spencer. Galeries Lafayette *(metro: Havre-Caumartin)*, in particular, has beautiful art nouveau décor. Nearby, the **Musée Grévin**, *10 boulevard Montmartre, 9th (metro: Montmartre)*, is a waxworks museum inspired by Madame Tussaud's and beloved by children.

At the crossroads of six boulevards, in the Place de l'Opéra *(metro: Opéra)* sits Napoleon III's magnificently pompous **Opéra Garnier** (after the architect, Charles Garnier), which opened in 1875. The design is a hotch-potch of grandiose styles, covered in relief busts of famous musicians, classical columns and baroque statuary. Inside, Garnier used multi-coloured marble from every quarry in France, more statues and lashings of gold leaf. The unexpected highlight, however, is painter Marc Chagall's glorious, swirling ceiling under the dome, painted in 1964. Astonishingly, the largest theatre in the world can only seat 2200 people. The rest is taken up by a vast stage and endless galleries and basements of dressing rooms, wardrobes, and workshops which provided the subterranean inspiration for Gaston Leroux's *Fantôme de l' Opéra*, about the horribly deformed phantom who lurks beneath the theatre and falls in love with a young singer. There is a small museum in the Imperial Pavilion.

The magnificent central glass dome of Galeries Lafayette adds a special sense of occasion to shopping.

6
North-West Paris: the Rive Droite

Place de la Concorde **

This cavernous square *(metro: Concorde)*, laid out in 1755–75 by Jacques-Ange Gabriel for Louis XV, was designed as a promenade – hard to imagine as you dodge the swirling, lethal traffic. It is built up only on one side, with two supremely elegant colonnaded buildings; the Hôtel de la Marine (right), and one of Paris' most luxurious hotels, the Hôtel Crillon (left). To the east are the Tuileries (see page 63); to the south, the river. To the west, copies of Coustou's superb 18th-century Marly horses mark the entrance to the Champs-Elysées (the originals are in the Louvre for safe-keeping).

The huge central octagon has a statue at each point representing great cities of France (clockwise from the bridge: Bordeaux, Nantes, Brest, Rouen, Lille, Strasbourg, Lyons, and Marseilles). Within it are two huge, ornate 19th-century bronze fountains, dripping with bearded gods, mermaids and fish, by Jacques Hittorff, and the 75m (250ft) granite **obelisk**, carved in Luxor *c*1250BC and given to France by Muhammed Ali, the Ottoman governor of Egypt, in 1829. The **Pont de la Concorde** was completed in 1791 using stones from the newly demolished Bastille.

In 1770, during the wedding celebrations of the Dauphin and Marie-Antoinette, a stand collapsed killing 133 people. During much of the Revolution, the Place became home to the Guillotine. Both Louis XVI and Marie-Antoinette were beheaded here. It was given its eventual name of Concorde as a gesture of reconciliation.

WALK

Start in the Place de la Concorde. Turn right, cross the Cours la Reine and drop down onto the quay. Walk past the houseboat colony to Pont Alexandre III. Climb up, take Av. Churchill, between the Grand and Petit Palais and turn left onto the Champs-Elysées. At Rond Point, turn left onto Av. Montaigne and follow this to Place de l'Alma (with metro and Bâteau Mouche stops). Alternatively, take Av. George V back up to the Champs-Elysées and turn left for the Arc de Triomphe, or right for the Place de la Concorde.

Opposite: *The huge Place de la Concorde has magnificent statuary and fountains.*

1. Arc de Triomphe
2. Place de l'Etoile
3. Palais d'Elysée
4. Grand Palace
5. Petit Palace
6. Pont Alexandre III
7. Place de la Concorde
8. Place de la Madeleine
9. Palais de Chaillot
10. Musée Guimet
11. Musée d'Art Moderne de la Ville de Paris
12. Musée de la Mode et de la Costume
13. Pont de l'Alma
14. Palais Bourbon
15. Musée D'Orsay
16. Hôtel des Invalides
17. Ecole Militaire
18. Eiffel Tower
19. Place d'Iena

Rue Royale, leading north, is one of the richest and most exclusive shopping streets in Paris, a joy for people-watchers and window-shoppers. At no 9, above the **Bouilhet-Christofle** showroom, is a small museum dedicated to 150 years of silverware. At the far end, in the Place de la Madeleine *(metro: Madeleine)*, the **Eglise de La Madeleine** has confused history and architecture. Work started on the church in 1764 and again in 1777. The half-built site mouldered throughout the Revolution, until, in 1806, Napoleon commissioned Vignon to build the existing Greek temple as a Temple of Glory. In 1815 the Bourbons decided to turn it back into a church. The starkly classical exterior, surrounded by 52 Corinthian columns and a carved frieze, contrasts sharply with the ornately decorated Baroque opulence of the interior.

The Champs-Elysées

In 1667 Louis XIV and Le Nôtre laid out a promenade, straight on from the Tuileries, through fields of sheep and cows. Extended several times over the next century, a drive through these 'Elysian Fields' gradually came to be a popular outing. The real transformation began when Napoleon chose the hilltop for a triumphal arch.

Today the Champs-Elysées is heavily built up with offices and shops, overpriced cinemas, clubs and cafés and few feel inspired to linger lovingly. Only the first short section, from Concorde to the Rond Point, remains at all Elysian, flanked by mature trees and parkland.

Just off to the right, on av Marigny, the **Palais d'Elysée** is the official home of the President of France. To the left, the truly vast **Grand Palais** and not quite so vast **Petit Palais**, av Winston

> ### THE GRAND PARADES
>
> In 1810 a grand parade was held on the Champs-Elysées to mark the wedding of Napoleon and his second wife, Marie-Louise. The Arc de Triomphe was still under construction, so a canvas replica was hastily erected. In 1840 Napoleon's body was paraded here on its return from St Helena, and in 1871 the Germans marched to proclaim the end of the Franco-Prussian War. The French held massive Victory parades here in 1919 and 1944, to mark the end of each World War. There are now parades every Bastille Day (14 July) and Armistice Day (11 November); and it marks a key stage of the great bicycle race, the Tour de France.

No longer a rural prome nade, the Champs Elysées is now a bustling thorough-fare by day and night.

Cherub riding a dolphin on the Pont Alexandre III.

MINOR ART MUSEUMS

Atelier-Musée Henri Bouchard, 25 rue de l'Yvette, 16th (metro: Jasmin). The studio museum of sculptor Henri Bouchard (1875-1960).

Musée de Boulogne-Billancourt, 26 av André Morrizet, Boulogne-Billancourt (metro: Marcel Sembat). Dedicated to local artists and building design.

Musée Dapper, 50 av Victor Hugo, 16th (metro: Victor Hugo) Regular exhibitions of the finest African art.

Musée National Jean-Jaques Henner, 43 av de Villers, 17th (metro: Monceau). Over 700 paintings and drawings by Henner (1829-1905).

Musée Gustave Moreau, 14 rue de la Rochefoucauld, 9th (metro: Trinité). Symbolist painter Moreau (1825-98) lived and worked in this studio, now filled with thousands of his works.

Churchill *(metro: Champs Elysées-Clemenceau)* caused a sensation with their innovative use of glass and iron during the Universal Exhibition of 1900. Today the Petit Palais houses the **Musée des Beaux-Arts de la Ville de Paris**, full of sumptuous medieval, Renaissance and 18th-century furniture and *objets d'art* and an inspiring collection of 19th-century French paintings. The Grand Palais houses a conference centre, part of the University of Paris, and regular touring exhibitions. To the rear, the **Palais de la Découverte**, av. Franklin D. Roosevelt, was transformed for the 1937 Exhibition. Until the opening of the Cité des Sciences (see page 58), this was the premier science museum in Paris. It now seems a little faded, but is still fascinating with plenty of entertaining hands-on experiments.

The spectacular **Pont Alexandre III**, named after the Czar of Russia who laid the foundation stone in 1896, was also built for the 1900 Exhibition. It is the most beautiful of all the Paris bridges, a joyous affirmation of the Belle Epoque, flamboyant with cherubs, lions, garlands of flowers, birds, shells and shields. Below is a thriving colony of houseboats.

Avenue Montaigne is the global heart of haute couture, home to many of the world's greatest designers (see page 121). Most also have other outlets handling the real money-makers of prêt-à-porter (ready-to-wear), perfume and make-up. Couturier fashion is little more than a glamorous loss-leader these days.

The top of the hill is crowned by one of the city's most familiar icons. In 1806 Napoleon commissioned Chalgrin to design the massive Roman-style **Arc de Triomphe** *(metro: Charles de Gaulle-Etoile; access by subway)* as a celebration of his military victories. Fifty metres (165ft) high and 45m (150ft) wide, it was still incomplete when the Emperor was toppled, and was finally finished only in 1836 under his nephew, Louis-Philippe. At ground level are four high-relief sculptures, the finest of which, from the Champs-Elysées, are Rudes' *Departure of the Volunteers* in 1792, commonly known as the *Marseillaise* (right), and Cortot's *Triumph of 1810*, celebrating the Treaty of Vienna (left). The frieze above also depicts moments of Napoleonic glory, while the arch is inscribed with the names of 660 generals and 128 battles of the Empire. Beneath it lies the tomb of the Unknown Soldier. Stairs and a lift lead up to the roof, from where there are magnificent views. Inside is a small museum.

In 1854, Haussmann surrounded the Arc by a circle of twelve broad avenues, naming his creation the **Place de l'Etoile**. After World War II it was officially renamed **Place Charles de Gaulle**, but the name is rarely used.

AUTEUIL AND PASSY

Quiet, leafy and exclusive, the gilded great of Paris live firmly behind closed doors in this largely residential corner of Paris. Lively it is not, but it does have an extraordinary number of small museums.

Chief amongst them is the vast **Palais de Chaillot**, *place du Trocadéro, 16th (metro: Trocadéro)*, built for the 1937 Exhibition. The dramatic terraces in front of the building's hawklike wings offer the best possible view of the Eiffel Tower as well as a perfect skateboard slalom course. Inside, the **Musée de la Marine** houses numerous models of famous French ships, as well as parts of the real thing, instruments and paintings; the **Musée des Monuments Français**, founded originally by Viollet-le-

A symbol of France's battles, victories and freedom, the Arc de Triomphe is the starting point for the celebratory annual parade down the Champs Elysées on 14 July.

DON'T MISS

*** **The Arc de Triomphe:** less interesting than famous, you have to do it once
*** **The Palais de Chaillot**: the museums are interesting but the views are superb.

*The Palais de Chaillot is
built as two curved wings
either side of a terrace and
adorned with the work of
many sculptors.*

Duc, has thousands of models of famous French buildings, for those without the time or inclination to see the
originals. The **Musée de l'Homme** is an extraordinary if
somewhat dry and dusty anthropological collection,
including a particularly interesting African Cultural
Gallery. The **Musée de Cinéma Henri Langlois** is the
capital's unfortunately static homage to moving pictures,
with a treasure-trove of film memorabilia, only a fraction
of which is on show.

Nearby, the **Musée des Arts Asiatiques Guimet**, *6
place d'Iéna, 16th (metro: Iéna)*, has a superb collection of
Asian art, lush with ivory and temple bronzes, puppets
and masks, Chinese porcelain and jade. The **Musée d'Art
Moderne de la Ville de Paris**, in the Palais de Tokyo, *11
av du Président Wilson, 16th (metro: Alma-Marceau)*, kicks
off triumphantly with Raoul Dufy's *La Fée Electricité*, the
largest picture in the world, created, like the building
itself, for the 1937 Exhibition. Numerous other modern
masters make this a fitting companion to the Pompidou
Centre. The **Musée de la Mode et de la Costume**, in the
Palais Galliera, *10 av Pierre 1er de Serbie, 16th (metro: Iéna,
Alma-Marceau)*, has some 16,000 costumes and textiles,
shown in constantly changing exhibitions, to protect the
fragile cloth. The **Musée Marmottan**, *2 rue Louis-Boilly,
16th (metro: La Muette)*, is a family collection with several
superb Monets and other Impressionists as well as
medieval and Napoleonic furniture and art, and a magnificent collection of illuminated manuscripts.

NORTH OF THE CHAMPS-ELYSEES

Another cluster of museums is centred on **Place St-Augustin**, with its huge 19th-century church and statue of Jeanne d'Arc. **Musée Jacquemart-André**, *158 boulevard Haussmann, 8th (metro: St-Philippe-du-Roule, Miromesnil)*, has a wonderful display of Italian Renaissance and 17th–18th century Flemish and French art. Look out for works by Donatello, Botticelli, Della Robbia, Tiepolo, Bernini, Rembrandt, Watteau, Boucher, Reynolds and Van Dyck. The **Musée Cernuschi**, *7 av Vélasquez, 8th (metro: Monceau, Villiers)*, concentrates solely on Chinese art through the ages. The **Musée de Nissim de Camondo**, *63 rue Monceau, 8th (metro: Villiers, Monceau)*, has a superb collection of carpets, 18th-century furniture and *objets d'art*.

Further north still, at *59 av Foch, 16th (metro: Porte Dauphine)*, are the **Musée Arménien**, dedicated to Armenian arts, manuscripts and jewellery and the **Musée National d'Ennery** of Far Eastern art, including a fine collection of Japanese netsukes. The **Musée de la Contrefaçon**, *16 rue de la Faisanderie, 16th (metro: Porte Dauphine)*, has a totally fascinating catalogue of fakes and forgeries, from 200BC to the present day. The **Musée des Lunettes et des Lorgnettes**, *2 av Mozart, 16th (metro: La Muette)*, has everything from spectacles to binoculars and is surprisingly interesting.

The 19th-century church of St Augustin was built on an iron framework by Baltard, who was also responsible for building the pavilions of Les Halles.

7
The Eiffel Tower, Les Invalides and the Musée d'Orsay

Eiffel Tower ***

quai Branly (metro: Bir-Hakeim; RER: Champs-de-Mars, Tour Eiffel)

There are usually massive queues; arrive early and expect to wait. Wishing to mark the centenary of the Revolution in spectacular fashion, the organizers of the 1889 Exhibition looked at literally thousands of projects before settling, amidst a hail of protests, on engineer Gustave Eiffel's iron tower. Work began in 1887 and was completed in time for its official opening on 31 March 1889. The 320.75m (1051ft) high tower sits on four feet, forming a 125m (415ft) square so perfectly balanced that the pressure never exceeds more than 4kg per cm², the weight of a seated man. It weighs 9550 tonnes of iron, contains 15,000 pieces of metal and 2.5 million rivets. There are 1652 steps to the third level (or, thankfully, Eiffel's original hydraulic lifts), from which, on a clear day, you can see up to 70km (45 miles). Originally it was painted in graduated colours, from a deep bronze at the base to a pale yellow at the top. In 1909, when Gustave Eiffel's highly profitable 20-year ticket concession came to an end, the tower received a last-minute reprieve from demolition in the interests of science. In 1914 it was commissioned as a transmitter, playing a vital role in the conduct of the war. In 1916 it became the beacon for the trans-atlantic radio-telephone service. Messages intercepted here led to the arrest of Mata Hari in February 1917. On 30 December 1921 it launched French civil broadcasting and in 1925 Citroën used it as the frame for

Opposite: *A feat of engineering, the Eiffel Tower was erected in the Champ-de-Mars, scene of great jubilation on the Revolution's first centenary.*

Opposite: A gilded dome crowns the Eglise du Dôme of Les Invalides. Commissioned by Louis XIV, it became the burial place of Napoleon.

the world's largest illuminated sign. Today, it is a meteorological and aircraft navigation station, and television and radio transmitter. Little models of the metal monster are the single most popular souvenir of the city. Until 1930 it remained the tallest building in the world. A small museum on the first stage tells the story of the tower, including some of its most famous visitors and the numerous lunatic and often fatal stunts it has

1. Eiffel Tower
2. Champ de Mars
3. Musée Rodin
4. Hôtel des Invalides
5. Musée de l'Armée
6. Musée de l'Ordre
7. Musée de la Seita
8. Pont Alexandre III
9. Palais Bourbon & Assemblée Nationale
10. Ecole Militaire
11. UNESCO Building
12. Musée d'Orsay

inspired. Above all, the tower has become the icon of Paris, an international symbol which would surely gladden the hearts of that 1889 committee.

Stretching back from the tower, the **Champ de Mars** began life as a military parade ground. In 1790 Louis XVI was reluctantly brought along to celebrate the first anniversary of the taking of the Bastille and in 1794 Robespierre held a massive festival here in honour of the Supreme Being and the immortality of the soul. Lighter entertainments have included balloon ascents, early flying machines, horse races and, during the Great Exhibitions, such diverse attractions as a train that ran on a cushion of water and a 70m (230ft) electric fairy. At the far end, the **Ecole Militaire**, *13 place Joffre, 7th (metro: Ecole Militaire)*, is an elegant and architecturally important Classical building designed by Jacques-Ange Gabriel in 1751, on the instigation of Madame de Pompadour. The aim of the military school was to train those with no money but good officer potential; its most famous graduate was Napoleon. Just behind this is the Y-shaped **UNESCO Building**, *7 place de Fontenoy, 7th (metro: Ségur, Cambronne)*, home of the United Nations Educational, Scientific, and Cultural Organization and an international treasure-trove of modern art, including works by Henry Moore, Miró, Le Corbusier and Picasso.

WALK

The lengthy Rue de l'Université runs from St-Germain-des-Prés to the Eiffel Tower. As you move west, the feeling changes from the bustling, villagey atmosphere of the Left Bank to the sophisticated and self-contained emotions of the chic 7th arrondissement. Street life gives way to the closed portes cochères of the grand hôtels, many of which are now ministries or embassies.

The residential Rue St Dominique, between the Invalides and the Champ de Mars, is also a pleasant stroll with wonderful views of the Eiffel Tower. Small food shops are interspersed with clothes, flowers and household goods, and it is a good hunting ground for *dégriffés* garments. Look for the neo-classical Fontaine de Mars and, at no 12, the wonderful Art Nouveau Liceo Italiano. Just off it, the well-heeled clientèle of the charming Rue Cler market is reflected in the quality of the merchandise.

Hôtel des Invalides **

rue de Grenelle, 7th (metro: Varenne, Latour-Maubourg, Invalides).

Another huge ceremonial esplanade, laid out in 1720, leads from Pont Alexandre III (see page 72) to this massive complex, built in 1670–76 by Louis XIV as a veterans' hospital. Designed by Libéral Bruand, it centres on the **Cour d'Honneur**, inspired by the Escorial in Madrid, and housed 6000 men. On 14 July 1789 the mob broke in and stole 28,000 rifles, which they used in the attack on the Bastille. It was the first violent act of the Revolution. Behind the court, the austere **Eglise de St-Louis-des-Invalides** is hung with the flags and standards of France, and those captured from the enemy. The collection is

RIVERS OF SLUDGE

Until Baron Haussmann got going in 1852, aided by an engineer, Balgrand, Paris had only the most rudimentary drains and was renowned for the filth of its streets. Today, there are 2050km (1274 miles) of tunnel, nearly 6m (20ft) high and 4m (13ft) across, with 26,000 manholes. The Parisians are so proud of their Sewers that since 1867 they have offered tours (*93 quai d'Orsay, 7th; metro: Pont de l'Alma*). Boat cruises were discontinued after someone used one in a successful bank robbery; now tours consist of a film, small museum and short walk.

thinner than it might have been; 1417 were incinerated by the governor in 1814, to save them from the clutches of the advancing Allies. The glittering gold **Eglise du Dôme** (1677–1735) was designed by Hardouin-Mansart as a royal chapel. Several military heroes of France are buried here, but they sink into obscurity beside the splendid **tomb of Napoleon**. He was buried here in 1840, 19 years after his actual death on St Helena, encased in seven coffins, of iron, mahogany, lead (two), ebony, oak and the outer tomb of porphyry, surrounded by the names of his most famous victories. The tomb is viewed from the balcony, it is said, to ensure that you bow your head to the Emperor. Look for the stiff-necked, squinting Englishmen trying to peek without submitting!

The entrance to the **Musée de l'Armée** is marked by an old taxi, homage to the taxi drivers who ferried 7000 troops to the Battle of the Marne in 1914, saving Paris from invasion. This is one of the largest military collections in the world, with over 10,000 uniforms, including Henry II's armour, Napoleon's coat, military paintings and a seemingly endless supply of arms, many of artistic value. Look out for Napoleon's death mask; also his favourite dog and favourite horse, both stuffed. Still in Les Invalides, the **Musée des Plans-Reliefs** is a collection of beautiful scale models of fortified towns, started by Louis XIV in 1686. The last was added in 1870, but they remained an official secret until 1927.

Cannon on display at the Hôtel des Invalides. A military arsenal was kept here before the Revolution.

Tucked behind a high wall, a few minutes' walk away, is the superb **Musée Rodin**, *77 rue de Varenne, 7th (metro: Varenne)*. Unlike so many of his contemporaries, Auguste Rodin (1840–1917) became such a success during his lifetime that he was offered the beautiful Hôtel Biron on condition that he left his work to the state. The resulting museum is small and immensely satisfying. The elegant salons and delightful gardens of the mansion built by Gabriel and Aubert (1731) are filled by a superb body of work by the master sculptor, including such famous pieces as *The Kiss, The Thinker, The Burghers of Calais* and the magnificent, harrowing

The iron-framed Gare d'Orsay has been converted into a light, spacious art gallery giving prominent display to the work of the Impressionists.

Gates of Hell. Real fans should also visit Rodin's studio in the Villa des Brillants, Meudon.

The Rue de Varenne, which connects Invalides with the wealthy residential Faubourg St-Germain, has a number of fine hôtels, chief amongst them the **Hôtel Matignon** (no 57), official residence of the Prime Minister. At the far end is the **Fontaine de Quatre Saisons**, carved by Bouchon between 1739 and 1745. From here, Rue de Luynes runs past the baroque **Eglise de St-Thomas d'Aquin** to the Musée d'Orsay.

Musée d'Orsay ★★★

1 rue de Bellechasse, 7th (metro: Solférino; RER: Musée d'Orsay)

The cavernous glass and iron Gare d'Orsay, built by Victor Laloux for the 1900 Exhibition, was once the most

La Siesta by Van Gogh (1853–90) in the Musée d'Orsay. In 1886 the artist arrived in Paris, where he was influenced by the colours and attitudes of the Impressionist painters.

IT'S A SCANDAL

When Manet's *Déjeuner sur l'Herbe* was exhibited at the Salon des Refusés in 1863 it caused a scandal. Based on Giorgione's *Concert champêtre*, Manet (1832–83) had produced a painting in the academic tradition in which he had trained, yet the official Salon rejected it. It was Manet's work, however, that inspired Monet and the other Impressionists, although Manet himself never exhibited with them. He continued to paint his subjects by emphasizing the contrast between light and dark tones, in which the use of black played an important part, rather than trying to convey his visual impressions. It was only late in his life that he took to painting outdoors and to using the 'rainbow palette' that excluded black.

central of Paris's ring of railway stations. Saved at the last minute from the crusher's ball, it re-opened in 1986, beautifully converted into a truly spectacular museum of art from 1848 to 1914, the period when Paris swept the world. A sculpture gallery runs through the heart of the museum, flanked by three floors of smaller galleries, showing the development of style from the ground up, with works by Ingres, Delacroix and Corot. The undoubted highlight is the magnificent Impressionist collection, which feels like the best sort of party, filled with old friends – from *Whistler's Mother* to the self-portraits by Cézanne and Van Gogh. Many of the world's most famous paintings are here, including Manet's *Olympia* and *Déjeuner sur l'Herbe*, which heralded the arrival of the Impressionist movement. Don't ignore some of the more unusual exhibits, including a room of delightful Toulouse-Lautrec pastels, furniture by Mackintosh and Frank Lloyd Wright, satirical sketches and an architecture gallery. If you only ever visit one museum, this must be the one.

A little way along the quay, the **Palais Bourbon**, *126 rue de l'Université, 7th (metro: Assemblée-Nationale)*, stares across the river at the Place de la Concorde (see page 69). Built in 1722–8 for Louis XIV's daughter, the palace has a classical façade, added by Poyet on Napoleon's orders in 1807. Since 1827 it has been home to the French parliament, the Assemblée Nationale.

Portrait *by Cézanne (1839–1906) in the Musée d'Orsay. Cézanne's work was exhibited at the first Impressionist exhibition in 1874.*

OTHER MUSEUMS IN THE AREA

The **Musée de la Seita**, *12 rue Surcouf, 7th (metro: Invalides, Latour-Maubourg)*, opened for the 1937 Exhibition, is dedicated to the history of tobacco and smoking.

The **Musée de la Légion d'Honneur**, *2 rue de Bellechasse, 7th (metro: Solférino; RER: Musée d'Orsay)*, has a collection of military medals and decorations. It is named after Napoleon's highest order, inaugurated in 1802, and adjoins the **Palais de la Légion d'Honneur**. This 18th-century palace was built for a German prince who fell on hard times and was forced to sell the mansion and rent it as a tenant. After the Revolution it was raffled off. Later it was the home of Mme de Staël, whose salon became a focus for many of the intellectuals of the time.

The **Musée de l'Ordre de la Libération**, *51bis boulevard de Latour-Maubourg, 7th (metro: Latour-Maubourg)*, commemorates the French during World War II, particularly the Free French and recipients of France's highest military honour, created by De Gaulle in 1940.

LES EXPOSITIONS UNIVERSELLES

In 1855, 1867, 1878, 1889, 1900, 1925 and 1937 Paris held a series of World Fairs which sent the city's reputation sparkling across the world and left it with a number of spectacular additions. Popular inventions promoted here included silver plate, the saxophone, the telephone, phonograph, television, and ice-making machine, and early automobiles ... the list goes on and on. In 1855 Queen Victoria became the first British monarch to visit France since 1431. In 1889, the centenary of the Revolution, the star turn was the Eiffel Tower. In 1900 the exhibition created the flamboyant Pont Alexandre III, the Grand and Petit Palais (see page 71) and the Gare d'Orsay (see page 81).

8
The Rive Gauche and Montparnasse

St-Germain-des-Pres and Luxembourg

From the 7th century onwards, the area around St-Germain-des-Prés was totally dominated by its powerful Benedictine abbey, which remained effectively independent from the city, cultivating a sophisticated cosmopolitan atmosphere that survives until today. The development of the highly aristocratic and expensive Faubourg St Germain assured it a place halfway between old money and radical chic. The Comédie Française flourished on the Rue de l'Ancienne Comédie until forced out by puritanical university officials in 1688 and the area had a famous month-long fair. In 1857 **Eugène Delacroix** set up his studio at 6 rue Fürstenburg, now a small museum dedicated to the Romantic painter. Following World War II, the ever-mobile artists' colony, now led by the writers Sartre and de Beauvoir, moved north from Montparnasse (see page 93), settling into cafés like *Les Deux Magots*, the *Brasserie Lipp*, the *Café de Flore* and most historic of all, *Le Procope*, which claims to be the world's oldest coffee house, founded in 1686. Famous customers have included Voltaire, Oscar Wilde, Napoleon, Victor Hugo and Joseph Guillotin (1743–93), who perfected his killing machine on sheep in the nearby Cours de Rohan. Today, the area is filled with ultra-expensive apartments, trendy people, and the shops in which they love to spend. Its pavements are tarred because the students tore up the cobbles and hurled them at police during the May 1968 revolt, a fact commemorated in a pavement sculpture on Place St-Germain-des-Prés.

WALK

From Place St-Germain-des-Prés, walk down Rue Bonaparte, through Place St Sulpice, emerging on Rue de Vaugirard. Enter the Jardins du Luxembourg; leave on the far side, on Boulevard St Michel. Turn left, then right onto Rue Soufflot for the Panthéon. Walk back down Rue Soufflot. Halfway along, turn right onto Rue St Jacques. Turn left onto Rue des Ecoles and right onto Rue de Cluny for the Musée de Cluny; left for Boulevard St Germain. Cross and take Rue Boutebrie. At the top, turn left for Place St Michel and the metro.

Opposite: *Accordionist in the Latin Quarter.*

1. St-Germain-des-Prés
2. Institut de France & Hôtel des Monnaies
3. Eglise de St Séverin
4. Eglise de St Julien-le-Pauvre
5. La Sorbonne
6. Panthéon
7. Musée de Cluny
8. Musée de la Préfecture de Police
9. Palais du Luxembourg
10. Jardin du Luxembourg
11. Eglise St Sulpice
12. Val de Grâce
13. Ecole Nat. Supérieur des Mines
14. Institut du Monde Arabe
15. Mosquée de Paris
16. Jardin des Plantes
17. Musée de Minéralogie
18. Musée National d'Histoire Naturelle
19. Musée de Sculpture en Plein Air
20. Observatoire de Paris

The **Eglise de St-Germain** opposite *(metro: St-Germain-des-Prés)* was founded by King Childebert in 542 to house several priceless relics, including a fragment of the True Cross, and was later named after the bishop of Paris at the time. Sacked four times by Normans in the 9th century, the earliest surviving sections date back to 866, making it the oldest church in Paris, although most of it was rebuilt in 1193. The abbey remained rich and powerful until the Revolution, when it was virtually destroyed and its priceless library confiscated. The mid-19th century restorers mangled a lot of what was left.

To the north, along the river, the **Musée de la Monnaie**, *11 quai de Conti, 6th (metro: St-Michel, Odéon)*, is housed in the old national mint, moved here by Louis XV in 1775. The museum, dedicated to cash, is surprisingly interesting and it is also possible to tour the medal workshops. Close by are also the **Institut de France**, home to five academies including the prestigious Académie

In the square outside the church of St-Sulpice stands a fountain commemorating four French bishops – Bossuet, Fénelon, Massillon and Fléchier.

Française and the Académie des Sciences; and the **Ecole Nationale des Beaux-Arts**.

To the south, work on the huge Baroque **Eglise de St-Sulpice** *(place and metro: St-Sulpice)*, dedicated to a 7th-century archbishop of Bourges, began in 1646. Many architects, including Le Vau and Gittard, worked on it but the grandiose façade was added a century later by Florentine architect, Servandoni. The south tower was never finished. Inside are several fine 19th-century frescoes, including works by Delacroix, an 18th-century astronomical gnomon, which marks the seasons and the hours of sunrise, and a magnificent organ (1781). In the square is the 1844 **Fontaine des Quatre Evêques**. Round

DON'T MISS

★★★ **The Musée de Cluny**: the superb French National collection of medieval art, including the Lady and the Unicorn tapestries
★★★ **The Panthéon**: a cavernous ex-church full of heroes of France
★★★ **Latin Quarter**: cheerful alleys and cheap restaurants, oozing atmosphere.

Right: *Ponies wait patiently to give rides in a wintry Jardins du Luxembourg.*

Opposite: *A fresh seafood restaurant displays its delicacies in the Latin Quarter.*

the corner, on Rue de Sèvres, is one of the great department stores of Paris, **Au Bon Marché**.

A little further on are the **Jardins du Luxembourg**, *boulevard St Michel, 6th (RER: Luxembourg)*, formal gardens lined with fine sculptures and uncomfortable benches. Originally created for Marie de Medici in 1613, they were re-landscaped by Chalgrin in the 19th century. Today, they are a regular student hang-out. At the north end, perfectly reflected in a pond popular with model boaters is the **Palais du Luxembourg**, again built for Marie and heavily altered by Chalgrin. It is now home to the Senate and is only open for visits to the gallery when the house is sitting.

Below: *The Latin Quarter. Its twisting streets and alleys are a multi-cultural hive of activity and interest.*

THE LATIN QUARTER ★★★
(metro: St Michel, Maubert-Mutualité, Cluny-La Sorbonne)
On the other side of **Boulevard St Michel**, the main shopping street in the area, is a rare surviving fragment of medieval Paris, home to students since the 13th century. Rabelais nicknamed it because Latin was the only language used in the university grounds until the 19th century. Today, its huddle of narrow winding streets are filled with a multi-cultural cornucopia of cheap and cheerful cafés, kebab shops, crêperies, buskers and bijou boutiques.

The **Eglise de St Séverin**, *3 rue Prêtres-St-Séverin, 5th*, is the official university church, named after either of two 6th-century saints, both of whom did favours for King Clovis. Rebuilt at regular intervals from the 6th century onwards, the existing church is largely 15th-century Gothic, with several magnificent Romanesque capitals, a double ambulatory springing from a twisting central column, and some fine modern stained glass. The Rococo organ (1745) was played by Fauré and Saint-Saëns. In 1474 a condemned murderer was offered his freedom if he survived an experimental operation for gallstones. It was carried out in the garden, then a charnel-house. Astonishingly, the patient lived to tell the tale.

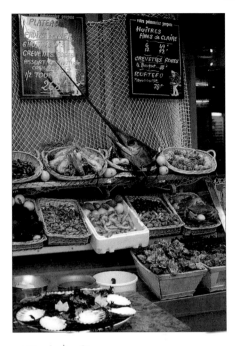

The little **Eglise de St-Julien-le-Pauvre**, *1 rue St-Julien-le-Pauvre, 5th*, was named after St Julian the Hospitaller who accidentally murdered his parents, and spent the rest of his life caring for the poor to make up for it. Built originally in the 6th century, it was largely rebuilt in the 13th century when it was used as an assembly hall for students. It was virtually destroyed during student riots in 1524, and rebuilt in 1651. Today, it is run by the Greek Orthodox Church.

Known universally as the Musée de Cluny, the **Musée National du Moyen Age**, *6 place Painlevé, 5th (metro: Cluny-La Sorbonne, St Michel, Odéon)* is housed in a magnificent mansion built *c*1500 by Jacques d'Amboise, Abbot of the Benedictine monastery founded here in the 1330s. Beside it are the **Thermes de Cluny**, 2nd-century AD Roman baths. Inside is the exquisite and superbly displayed national collection of medieval art and artefacts, founded by Alexandre de Sommerard in 1832. The state bought both the collection and the mansion in 1844. It is

---

HOTEL DE CLUNY

The Hôtel de Cluny, which houses the museum, is a fine example of a medieval domestic residence. The heraldic arms of the Amboise family surmount the archway that leads to its attractive courtyard and the house has had many illustrious inhabitants. The young Mary Tudor, sister of Henry VIII of England stayed here after the premature death of her much older husband, Louis XII of France. In the 17th century the mansion was the residence of the papal nuncios, including Mazarin.

Right: *The 15th-century Hôtel de Cluny is a fine example of a private mansion of the period and an appropriate setting for its superb collection of medieval art.*

Opposite: *The imposing 18th-century Panthéon is built in the Classical style. Formerly a church, it is the burial place of many of France's illustrious heroes.*

AL FRESCO FEASTS

The **Rue Mouffetard** (metro: Monge, Censier Daubenton) is the most famous market in Paris, with beautiful displays of exotic shellfish, heaps of gleaming lemons, North African spices, Italian cheeses, Greek vine leaves, Chinese dried mushrooms, French strawberries, olives and cheeses, gurgling vats of *choucroute* and spits of roasting chickens. Less well-known and equally atmospheric is the **Rue de Buci** (metro: St-Germain-des-Prés, Mabillon). Go in the early evening when the street is crowded with locals shopping for their evening meal.

a peerless treasure-trove of glittering gold crowns and reliquaries, smoothly rotund carvings in wood and ivory, glowing paintings, tapestries and stained glass, perfectly detailed illuminated manuscripts, stone capitals and heavy blackened furniture. In Salle VIII are the 28 heads of the Kings of Judea from Notre Dame (see page 35), beheaded in 1793 by Revolutionaries who believed them to be the kings of France. Salle XII, the barrel-vaulted frigidarium of the Roman baths, contains several Roman sculptures and altarpieces. Upstairs, in Salle XIII, the six sublime *millefleurs* tapestries depicting *La Dame à la Licorne* (the Lady and the Unicorn) were woven near Aubusson in the late 15th century and rescued from a dusty castle attic 400 years later.

In about 1127 Peter Abélard and his followers gathered to debate in the open air; in 1215 the University of Paris was eventually given official recognition. In 1253 Robert de Sorbon, chaplain to St Louis, founded **La Sorbonne**, for 16 poor theology students. It grew almost overnight into one of the great universities of the world, housed today in a sprawl of monumental 19th-century buildings, which stretch out behind the Rue des Ecoles and Boulevard St Michel.

Tucked in among them is the **Panthéon**, *place du Panthéon, 5th (metro: Luxembourg, Monge)*. The first abbey and church here was built in 508 by King Clovis, over St Geneviève's tomb. In 1757, in payment of a vow, Louis

XV began work on a new church for the glory of France, the monarchy and St Geneviève. In the shape of a Greek cross, topped by a huge dome and fronted by a classical peristyle, it was designed by Soufflot and completed in 1790, just in time for the Revolution. In 1791 it became a Pantheon for the heroes of the Republic. In November 1793 Revolutionaries melted down the saint's reliquary, burnt her remains and scattered the ashes on the Seine. Over the next century it became a political football, turning from pantheon to church and back again several times before it finally became a civil building in 1885. Along the way, almost every major artist of the establishment of the 19th century had a hand in painting frescoes and carving sculptures depicting the life of St Geneviève, the heroes and saints of France, the civic virtues, and the glorious Revolution. Foucault, inventor of the gyroscope, carried out scientific experiments here in 1851-2, suspending a pendulum from the dome to prove the earth's rotary motion. Heroes of France buried here include Voltaire, Victor Hugo, Jean-Jacques Rousseau, Emile Zola, the architect Soufflot, Louis Braille (inventor of Braille), Jean Moulin (leader of the French Resistance in World War II), René Cassin (author of the United Nations Declaration of Human Rights), and economist Jean Monnet (founder of the European Community).

Next door, the delightful little **Eglise de St-Etienne-du-Mont**, *place Ste-Geneviève, 5th (metro: Luxembourg, Monge)*, was founded in 1492. The basic structure is Gothic, but the foundation stone for the portal was laid in 1610, and the enchantingly light façade and much of the interior, particularly the glorious rood screen and pulpit, are pure Renaissance. The few relics of St Geneviève to survive the Revolution are now housed here as a focus of pilgrimage. The writers Pascal and Racine are buried here, as is the painter Le Sueur.

> **ST GENEVIEVE**
>
> Geneviève was a farmer's daughter, born in Nanterre in 422, who came to Paris and took holy orders. When Attila the Hun marched on the city in 451 Geneviève assured the terrified Parisians that they would be safe. When the Huns turned back without attacking her prophesy was hailed as a miracle. In 460 she built the first church over the tomb of St Denis (see page 99). On her death c500 her supposedly miraculous tomb became a popular place of pilgrimage and she was made patron saint of Paris, with her feast day on 3 January. The faithful prayed to her relics for three days before the Battle of the Marne in World War I and again the city was saved.

**SMALL AND
CURIOUS MUSEUMS**

**Collection Historique de la
Préfecture de Police**, *1bis
rue des Carmes, 5th (metro:
Maubert-Mutualité)*. An often
grisly collection of police
instruments and famous
clues.
**Musée de l'Assistance
Publique**, *47 quai de la
Tournelle, 5th (metro:
Maubert-Mutualité)*. French
hospitals since the Middle
Ages.
**Musée des Chasseurs à
pied, alpins, cyclistes**,
*Château de Vincennes
(metro: Vincennes)*.
Dedicated to walkers,
climbers and cyclists.
Musée de Curiosité, *11 rue
St-Paul, 4th (metro: St Paul)*.
Magic and illusion, complete
with magic shows.
**Musée de la Franc-
Maçonnerie**, *16 rue Cadet,
9th (metro: Cadet)*.
Freemasonry in France,
behind the Masonic temple.
Musée National de Sport,
*Parc des Princes, 24 rue du
Commandant-Guilbaud, 16th
(metro: Porte-St-Cloud)*.
Sporting memorabilia.

Jardin des Plantes Area

Stretched out along Quai St Bernard, the **Musée de
Sculpture en Plein Air** *(metro: Jussieu, Monge)* is an open-
air modern sculpture garden with works by Brancusi,
Zadkine and César. A little further along, the fascinating
Institut du Monde Arabe, *1 rue de Fossés St-Bernard, 5th
(metro: Jussieu, Cardinal Lemoine)*, was designed by Jean
Nouvel (1981) and paid for by the governments of France
and 22 Islamic countries. Its windows, based on Islamic
designs, have photo-electric shades which expand and
contract like the pupil of an eye, according to the amount
of available light. Inside is a superb museum of the
Islamic world, with art, architecture, furniture, jewellery,
and scientific and religious displays.

The **Jardin des Plantes** *(metro: Jussieu, Gare
d'Austerlitz)* was originally laid out as a medicinal herb
garden in 1626 by Jean Hérouard and Guy de la Brosse,
court physicians to Louis XIII. They also founded schools
of botany, natural history and pharmacy which have
mutated into a magnificent botanical garden. Buffon, the
naturalist, was superintendent here in 1739–88. Inside,
the **Musée National d'Histoire Naturelle**, *57 rue Buffon,
5th (metro: Gare d'Austerlitz)*, is filled with fossilized
plants, dinosaur bones, and lumps of rock.

In 1791 the last four surviving animals from the
Versailles menagerie were moved into the Garden. The
collection has grown, although most of the zoo's inhabitants were eaten during the 1870–1 siege. Today, it is a
pleasant little **zoo**, with large cats, bears and a wide vari-
ety of small animals and creepy-crawlies.

Behind the park the 1922 **Grande Mosquée de Paris**,
place du Puits-de-l'Ermite, 5th (metro: Monge), was built as
a memorial to the Muslims who died in World War I.
Today it is the cultural and religious headquarters of
some 3 million French Muslims. The fine courtyard is
modelled on the Alhambra.

Also nearby are the fascinating small **Musée de
Minéralogie**, Université Pierre et Marie Curie, *34 rue
Jussieu, 5th (metro: Jussieu)*, with a beautifully displayed
collection of gemstones and other minerals, and the 3rd-

century AD Roman **Arènes de Lutèce**, *rue des Arènes, 5th (metro: Cardinal Lemoine, Jussieu)*. The arena was destroyed by barbarians, rediscovered, and largely reconstructed in the 19th century.

MONTPARNASSE AND THE SOUTH

Montparnasse started life as a slag heap from the Roman quarries, nicknamed Mount Parnassus by students who gathered here for wine, women and poetry. From about 1800 onwards it attracted an increasingly large number of cafés and cabarets, but it really took off in the early 20th century as rents in Montmartre soared and the penniless artistic and intellectual community moved here en masse. Lenin, Trotsky, Hemingway, Gertrude Stein, Picasso and Eisenstein all worked and drank here. Tourists still flock to the area to breathe in the air of genius, but usually find only petrol fumes. The artists moved to St-Germain after the war and in the 1960s the area became the site of some horrendous 'new town' planning. Several of the famous cafés of the past survive, including **Le Sélect**, **Le Dôme**, **La Rotonde**, the **Closerie de Lilas** and **La Coupole**, where 30 artists contributed to the décor. Infinitely more expensive now, they are havens of warmth in a cold and uninviting concrete jungle.

It may look uninspiring, but the Tour Maine-Montparnasse offers a superb view of Paris and its environs.

At the heart of the new development soars the gigantic **Tour Maine-Montparnasse**, *33 av du Maine, 15th (metro: Montparnasse-Bienvenue)*; the tallest building in France, at 209m (700ft). There is a closed viewing platform on the 56th floor, and an open one on the 59th. On a clear day you can see up to 40km (25 miles). Post your cards here for a Tour Montparnasse frank.

Those interested in more than a mere postmark should visit the **Musée de la Poste**, *34 boulevard de Vaugirard, 15th (metro: Montparnasse-Bienvenue)*,

SARTRE AND DE BEAUVOIR

Jean-Paul Sartre and Simone de Beauvoir were life-long companions and two of the most influential thinkers of the 20th century. Sartre created the theory of Existentialism, which states that existence is basically futile, with no great purpose or meaning. You are totally free to mould and give value to your own life. Simone de Beauvoir's seminal work on the role of women, *The Second Sex* (1949), helped shape the thinking of the early Feminist movement and create a worldwide social revolution. Both were also highly entertaining writers, with a string of successful novels and plays.

LIBERTY

The US Statue of Liberty in New York Harbour, properly called 'Liberty enlightening the World', was given by France to the people of the USA to commemorate the centenary of American independence in 1886. Bartholdi's massive statue stands 67m (220ft) high, but a much smaller version of it can be seen in Paris at the extremity of the Ile des Cygnes in the midst of the river Seine, downstream past the Pont de Grenelle.

which has a magnificent stamp collection, and traces the history of the post from medieval parchments to the balloons and carrier pigeons used by besieged Parisians to relay messages in 1870.

Nearby, the **Cimetière de Montparnasse**, *3 boulevard Edgar Quinet, 14th (metro: Edgar-Quinet)*, is the third largest cemetery in Paris, founded in 1824. Its famous corpses include writers Jean-Paul Sartre (1905–80), Simone de Beauvoir (1908–86), Samuel Beckett (1906–89), Charles Baudelaire (1821–67) and Guy de Maupassant (1850–93); composers César Franck (1822–90) and Camille Saint-Saëns (1835–1921); sculptors Antoine Bourdelle (1861–1929), Ossip Zadkine (1890–1967), François Rude (1784–1855) and Frédéric Bartholdi (sculptor of the Statue of Liberty) (1834–1904); and André Citroën, founder of the car company.

For centuries, Parisian corpses were shoe-horned into a tiny corner of Les Halles (see page 40), but the body count rose out of control. In 1780 several people were asphyxiated by the smell. Something had to be done. Work began in 1786. It took 15 months to transfer an estimated two million bodies from the central cemeteries to an ancient quarry, which became known as the **Catacombs**, *place Denfert-Rochereau, 14th (metro: Denfert-Rochereau)*. Bones were stacked neatly on shelves, and skulls arranged in artistic heaps. The tourists flocked in; the aristocracy held parties and concerts; and the Resistance set up their headquarters in this unlikely place during World War II.

Nearby, the **Observatoire de Paris**, *61 av de l'Observatoire, 14th (metro: Denfert-Rochereau)*, was founded by Louis XIV in 1667 for the Académie des Sciences. It was designed by Claude Perrault on aesthetic rather than scientific principles, and early astronomers had to set up the telescope in the garden. It nevertheless became an important scientific centre, responsible for creating the metric system, discovering Neptune and calculating the exact circumference of the earth, the distance of the earth from the sun and the speed of light. Until 1884 it was the home of the Paris meridian, which vied with Greenwich

The Fontaine de l'Observatoire was designed by Davioud in 1873. Its magnificent rearing horses were sculptured by Frémiet.

as 0° longitude. It is still home to the Coordinated Universal Clock, official measure of French time.

The **Manufacture des Gobelins**, *42 av des Gobelins, 13th (metro: Gobelins)*, the famous Gobelins tapestry works, was founded in the early 17th century in an old dyeing factory. In 1662 Louis XIV annexed it and as a royal institution it became world renowned. At the same time the Gobelins took over the running of the royal carpet factory whose premises were a soapworks at Chaillot, hence the name Savonnerie. The Savonnerie was moved to the Gobelins site in the 19th century. In 1940 the Beauvais Tapestry moved here. You can watch workers manufacture traditional and modern designs and repair the priceless works of their forebears.

LES GOBELINS

The Gobelins factory is a fascinating place to visit and guided tours take you through the whole process and weaving of these magnificent tapestries. Artist-weavers undergoing study live on the premises and follow a long and thorough course of training in all aspects of weaving, dyeing and design. The tapestries are woven on looms, working from the reverse. The design to be followed is placed behind the weaver and the image is copied from its reflection in a mirror. Many of the designs are the work of well-known artists and the colour matching of yarn to paint is perfect. The tapestries now are mostly woven commissions to be given as diplomatic gifts by the French government.

9
The Suburbs

Bois de Boulogne **

(metro: Porte Maillot, Porte Dauphine, Porte d'Auteuil, Sablons; not safe at night).

Covering a massive 865ha (2000 acres), the Bois de Boulogne was a hunting preserve before it was enclosed in 1558 as a royal park. It became highly fashionable as a promenade and duelling ground when Louis XV opened it to the public, but it was only in 1852 that Baron Haussmann created a fully fledged public park after Napoleon III gave the area to the city. The Bois was modelled on London's Hyde Park, with winding walks. There are several distinct areas. The children's **Jardin d'Acclimation** has a playground, petting zoo, miniature railway, giant doll's house, bowling alley and an art gallery and workshop, the **Musée en Herbe**. The **Musée National des Arts et Traditions Populaires**, next door, has a fine rural crafts collection. The **Pré Catalan Area**, named after a 12th century Provençal minstrel murdered there, has a magnificent copper beech and a Shakespeare Garden, of plants mentioned in his plays. There are also two large boating lakes and particularly fine formal gardens in the **Jardin des Serres d'Auteuil** and the **Parc de Bagatelle**, which surrounds a delightful house built in 64 days in 1775 as a bet between Marie-Antoinette and the Comte d'Artois.

The most famous of the many amateur and professional sporting facilities are the **Roland Garros tennis stadium**, home of the French Open, and **Longchamps** (flat) and **Auteuil** (jump) racecourses.

DON'T MISS

*** **The Grande Arche de la Défense**: latest in a long line of monumental arches
*** **Malmaison**: the Empress Josephine's delightful château and rose garden.

Opposite: *The Bois de Boulogne offers an area of rural beauty and relaxation within a short distance of the centre of Paris.*

LA DEFENSE

A huge rebuilding programme planned to revitalize the inner suburbs, has taken place since the 1960s. The centre-piece, the **Grande Arche de La Défense** *(RER Line A: Grande Arche de la Défense)* is a gleaming white 100m (330ft) cube. It was designed by Danish architect, Johan Otto von Spreckelsen and inaugurated in 1989 to celebrate the Bicentennial of the Revolution. The sculptural canopy of 'clouds' is the work of British engineer Peter Rice. The views from the top are excellent.

On the **Parvis de la Défense**, the imaginative **Musée de l'Automobile** uses attractive multimedia displays and live performers to tell the history of the automobile, centred around 110 gleaming classic cars. In the bulbous **Dôme Imax**, the largest hemispherical screen in the world (1144m^2 [12,300 sq ft]) creates an overwhelming cinematic effect.

The Grande Arche de la Défense.

19th century Viollet-le-Duc carefully restored the Benedictine basilica of St Denis.

LA DEFENSE

La Défense is named after the 1870 defence of Paris. Work began on this ultra-modern business park, the largest construction project since the Maginot Line, in 1955. Designed to preserve the city centre from over-development, it has become a vast, soulless open esplanade, surrounded by tower blocks. Many were considered revolutionary in their day. Sadly, all too many now look tired, although some of the buildings and many of the scattered sculptures, by artists such as Miró and Calder, are interesting. About 35,000 people live here, and 100,000 work in its many offices.

MOBILE MARTYR

In AD262 St Denis, first bishop of Paris, finally went too far, desecrating several statues of Roman gods and emperors. He was arrested and beheaded on the Mont de Mercure (later renamed Montmartre in his honour). Defiant beyond the end, he picked up his head, tucked it under one arm, and strode off down the road. He finally stopped and was buried some 6km (4 miles) north, near the village of Catoliacus. St Denis is the patron saint of France.

ST-DENIS
Basilique de St-Denis*

place de la Légion d'Honneur (metro: St-Denis-Basilique).

As soon as St Geneviève built the first chapel over the tomb of St Denis in the 5th century, it became a popular pilgrimage centre. In the 7th century King Dagobert sponsored the foundation of a great royal abbey, which became the traditional burial place of kings. In 1144 Abbot Suger began work on a stunning new church, the first Gothic structure in France, completed by Pierre de Montreuil in the 13th century. Henry IV pragmatically renounced his Protestant beliefs here in 1593 in order to claim the throne of France. During the Revolution the church was desecrated and the royal corpses dumped in

Above: *The tombs of the kings of France in the basilica of St Denis.*

Opposite: *Detail from a tile in the Musée National de la Céramique, Sèvres.*

Below: *Malmaison became Josephine's home after her divorce from Napoleon.*

a communal grave. Astonishingly, the 79 tombs survived. Viollet-le-Duc restored the basilica in the 19th century.

The award-winning **Musée d'Art et d'Histoire**, *22bis rue Gabriel Péri*, is a 17th-century Carmelite convent with an excellent collection of fine and decorative arts, including many modern masterpieces, apothecaries' tools, local archaeology and a fascinating display on the 1871 Paris Commune. Meanwhile the rather shabby town is pouring millions of francs into exciting modern architectural projects, such as Oscar Niemeyer's 1989 headquarters for the magazine *L'Humanité*, and a new football stadium for the 1998 World Cup final.

OTHER SIGHTS

Malmaison *(RER line A to La Défense, then bus 158 to Bois Préau)*. In 1800 Napoleon and Josephine, aided by architects Percier and Fontaine, began to transform a rather ramshackle house into a residence fit for a Consul of France. The enchanting little château became Josephine's main residence after her divorce in 1809. The house is a fascinating record of the heyday of the Empire. Redouté, whose charming paintings of roses adorn the château walls, ladies' cloakrooms and table mats the world over, was among the staff who cherished Josephine's precious rose gardens. The **Château de Bois-Préau**, *1 av de l'Impératrice*, next door, houses a Napoleonic museum.

Vincennes *(metro: Porte Dorée, Château de Vincennes)*. From the 11th century the **Bois de Vincennes** was a royal hunting preserve. It became a military firing range in 1796 and a huge, supposedly English-style, park in 1860. The iris gardens are fabulous in season, but there is a general lack of interesting plants. To make up for this, there is a huge zoo and boating on Lake Daumesnil.

The no-nonsense **Château** (1337–80) comprises a solid keep and 15th–16th century copy of the Sainte-Chapelle (see page 32), surrounded by a formidable curtain wall and moat. In the early 17th century Le Vau added a new Résidence Royale, but Louis XIV turned the fortress into a prison. The castle has a colourful history – Henry V of England died in the keep, the Marquis de Sade and Mirabeau were imprisoned here and Mata Hari was shot here. Fouquet, who built Vaux-le-Vicomte, and upset Louis XIV, was also incarcerated here. There are three small museums, on the château's history, military insignia and mountaineering.

The fascinating **Musée des Arts d'Afrique et d'Océanie**, *293 av Daumesnil*, was built for the 1931 Exhibition as a celebration of the French colonies, but now houses a much wider anthropological collection from across Africa and the Pacific, and a tropical aquarium.

St Cloud and Sèvres, 10km (6 miles) west of Paris *(metro: Pont de Sèvres, Boulogne-Pont de St Cloud)*. Only Le Nôtre's delightful gardens, with their panoramic views of Paris and tumbling Grand Cascade of water terraces remain; Hardouin-Mansart's château (1675) was burnt to a crisp during the 1870 Siege of Paris. Napoleon staged his coup here on 9 November 1799. On the edge of the park are the **Manufacture de Sèvres**, home of fine porcelain since the 18th century, and the **Musée National de la Céramique**, *place de la Manufacture*, with thousands of ceramics from across the globe.

OTHER SIGHTS OF INTEREST

Le Centre Internationale de l'Automobile, *25 rue d'Estienne d'Orves, Pantin (metro: Hoche – Line 5)*. An enthusiast's dream collection of 100 cars. Famous motoring names include Ferrari, Ascari, Fangio and Jim Clark.
Le Château de Sceaux, 10km (6 miles) south-west of Paris *(RER Line B to Bourg-la-Reine)*. This mid-19th century pastiche of a château is home to the **Musée de l'Ile de France**. Le Nôtre's 17th-century gardens are magnificent.
Musée de l'Air et de l'Espace, *Le Bourget (RER Line B to Le Bourget or bus 350 from Gare de l'Est)*. Fascinating air museum with a collection of nearly 150 aircraft, at one of the world's great historic airports.
La Roseraie de l'Hay-les-Roses *(RER Line B to Bourg-la-Reine, then bus 192)*. The ultimate rose garden, created in 1892, with over 3000 species in 5km (3 miles) of flower beds.

10
The Ile de France

Disneyland Paris ★★★

A miniature version of its American parents, Disneyland is visited by over 10 million people each year. Four themed areas cluster round the towering spires of **Sleeping Beauty's Castle**. Start early and you can get round everything in one day.

Vintage cars and horse-drawn carriages ply **Main Street, USA** – small town East Coast America c1900 – which is also the route of the daily grand parades (usually late afternoon). Don't buy all your souvenirs in this concentration of shops and eateries, as each area has its own themed merchandise. Above the main entrance is the first of four stations of the **Disneyland Railroad**, a little steam train which chugs round the edge of the park.

Frontierland is yee-ha Wild West, with a Mark Twain riverboat steamer, a ghostly mansion, shooting gallery, and the scream-making Big Thunder Mountain roller-coaster among the rides and attractions.

In **Adventureland** are the Temple of Doom, tree-top home of the Swiss Family Robinson, an adventure island complete with rope walkways, Pirates of the Caribbean and Aladdin's Cave.

The cutely pastelled **Fantasyland**, home of Mickey, Pluto et al. is heartland of the Disney ideal and the best area for small children, with rides on Dumbo, a giant teacup, ferris wheel, toy train and merry-go-round, and gentle cruises through the fairy tales, past the children of the world, and the enchanting stories of Pinocchio, Snow White and Peter Pan.

OTHER THEME PARKS

France Miniature, Elancourt (*RER Line C to St-Quentin-en-Yvelines, then a shuttle bus*). Basically a giant map of France with waist-high miniatures of 166 of the country's top historical monuments and 15 typical regional villages.
Parc Astérix, Plailly (*RER Line B3 to Roissy, then a shuttle bus*). Popular theme park based on the cartoon adventures of Asterix the Gaul. The patriotic French are flocking here in preference to Disneyland.

Opposite: *Meet Goofy at Disneyland Paris.*

1 Big Thunder Mountain
2 Euro Disney Railroad
3 Phantom Manor
4 Main Street Station (Entrance)
5 Space Mountain
6 Videopolis
7 Le Visionarium
8 Star Tours
9 Snow White & Seven Dwarfs
10 Alice's Curious Labyrinth
11 Pirates of the Caribbean
12 Adventure Isle
13 Swiss Family Treehouse
14 Cottonwood Creek Ranch
15 Autopia (Futuristic Racetrack)

a Guest Parking
b Hotel Cheyenne
c Hotel Santa Fe
d Sequoia Lodge
e Newport Bay Club
f Lake Disney
g Buffalo Bill's Wild West Show
h Festival Disney
i Hotel New York
j Animal Care Centre
k RER Station-Marne-la-Vallée-Chessy
l Disneyland Hotel

300 m

300 yds

To Davy Crockett Ranch

Discoveryland is Disney's homage to science and probably the most interesting area for adults. Attractions include the Visionarium 'time-travel adventure', the Nautilus submarine, Discovery Mountain cannon, Star Tours (based on *Star Wars* effects) and a special Michael Jackson film presentation, *Captain Eo*.

Festival Disney provides themed evening entertainment, food and drink outside the main park. There is also a spectacular **Buffalo Bill Wild West Show** and barbecue every evening.

VERSAILLES ★★★

RER Line C5 to Versailles-Rive Gauche. Arrive early to beat the tour buses; plan carefully as different sections of the buildings open at different times and wear comfortable shoes for lots of walking. Allow time to visit the extensive gardens as well as the château.

Until 1661, when Fouquet was unwise enough to be more glamorous than the king (see page 110), Versailles was a simple hunting lodge. But Louis XIV really believed himself to be little short of divine and wanted a palace to match – bigger, better, more lavish and luxuriant than anyone else's. It took only 21 years for the architects Le Vau and Hardouin-Mansart to complete a palace whose sheer size, with its 680m (2250ft) long façade, leaves you gasping, although it was stripped of its furniture during the Revolution and many of the grandiose rooms are still very bare. While you wonder at the elaborate décor, you need imagination to repopulate this most glamorous of courts with up to 20,000 people including royalty, attendant aristocracy, government, foreign visitors, servants and even sightseers; anyone presentable was allowed to wander through and have a look, while the king got up and ready for bed in public and the poor queen even had her children with an audience.

The Château

Louis XIII's original lodge is just visible at the back of the **Cour de Marbre**, totally engulfed by the enormous wings. In the north wing are the sumptuous *faux marbre* private theatre, the **Opéra Royal**, finished in 1770 for the

---

THE SUN KING

Louis XIV (1643–1715) came to the throne in 1643, aged five, with his mother, Anne of Austria, as regent, but only to power after the death of Cardinal Mazarin in 1661. In 1660 he married Infanta Maria Theresa of Spain. He spent 38 years at war with Spain, the Netherlands, Alsace, southern Germany and Italy while his Chief Minister, Colbert, enforced endless pernickety laws, creating a total dictatorship. Above all, Louis is remembered as the flamboyant 'Sun King' who thought himself divine, identified with Apollo, created a glittering era of lavish spending and great art, and bled the country dry.

The site of Versailles was originally marshland; teams of workers were employed to level and drain the area.

1. Queen's Bedroom
2. Hall of Mirrors
3. King's Bedroom
4. Salon de la Guerre
5. Oeil-de-Boeuf
6. The Cabinet du Conseil
7. Salon d'Apollon
8. Salon d'Hercule
9. Entrance
10. Louis XVI's library
11. Salon de Venus
12. Salon du Sacre

State apartments
King's apartments
Madame de Maintenon's apartments
Queen's apartments
Coronation room

LE NÔTRE

André Le Nôtre (1613–1700) was the foremost French landscape gardener of the 17th century. Responsible for the gardens at Vaux-le-Vicomte, he was commissioned by Louis XIV to design the superb grounds of Versailles. Here he planned a masterpiece series of formal outdoor 'rooms', placing them against a backdrop of natural wooded areas, as an appropriate setting for the vast palace.

wedding of Louis XVI and Marie-Antoinette, Robert de Cotte's beautiful creamy Baroque **Chapelle Royale** (1710), and the elaborately gilded and decorated **Grands Appartements**, each dedicated to one of the Roman gods. The Salon d'Apollon was the throne room; the Salon de Mercure, the state bedroom; the Salon de Diane a games room; and the Salon de Mars a ballroom. All are heavily embellished. By far the most magnificent is the glittering 80m (260ft) long **Galerie des Glaces** (Hall of Mirrors), with 17 vast windows carefully arranged so that the sun's dazzling light would reflect off the mirrors and back outside, to make it seem as if the Sun King really did shine. It was here, in the aftermath of the Franco-Prussian War, that Bismarck made the Kaiser head of a united Germany, and here, in November 1919, that Germany signed the Treaty of Versailles, officially ending World War I.

From 1727 onwards, Louis XV, together with Jacques-Ange Gabriel, began to create the **Petits Cabinets**, charming rooms on a more human scale, which became the apartments of his powerful mistress, Madame du Barry. In 1738 he himself moved from the chilly state bedroom into a new suite of **Appartements du Roi**, filled with magnificent carvings by Verberkt. The **Appartements de la Reine**, designed originally for Marie-Leczinska in 1729, were in the south wing. They are now furnished as they would have been for Marie-Antoinette.

DON'T MISS

*** **Versailles**: Louis XIV's palace of palaces
*** **Disneyland Paris**: Disney's attempt to outstrip Louis XIV.

The Grounds

The magnificent gardens, recently restored to Le Nôtre's original 17th-century splendour, are vast. Directly in front of the château is a formal patterned terrace of lawns, fountains and pathways, studded by some 200 magnificent statues, many of which used to be gilded. Beyond this stretch the Grand and Petit Canals, which once had their own fleet of boats including gondolas and an orchestral barge, conducted by Lully.

To the right is the **Grand Trianon**. The first pavilion here was built as a trysting place where Louis XIV could meet his mistress, Madame de Montespan. The current building by Mansart (1687) became a private inner court to which only intimates and the highly favoured were invited. Carefully restored, it is now the most lavishly decorated of all the palace suites, giving a clear vision of the sumptuous life at court.

The ornate, lavishly gilded and rather public bedroom of the 'Sun King' Louis XIV at Versailles.

Another notorious royal mistress, Madame de Pompadour, kept Louis XV entertained from 1745–9, by building the New Menagerie, a glamorous farmyard centred on the **Pavillon Français**. In 1761 botanical gardens were laid out in the surrounding area, though later changed to the less formal English style preferred by Marie-Antoinette.

In 1763 work began on the **Petit Trianon**, an almost perfect, deceptively simple little classical palace, designed by Jacques-Ange Gabriel. Louis XVI gave this to his charming and frivolous wife, Marie-Antoinette (1755–93) who spent her happiest moments here with a small, informal group of intimates. She also spent vast amounts of money remodelling the surrounding gardens into artificial countryside, and building a model village and farmhouse, the **Hameau**, where she and her ladies-in-waiting would wander dressed as milkmaids. Labourers were employed for the real farm work at the dairy and mill. The Queen was near here when the Revolutionary mob attacked the palace.

OTHER SIGHTS OF INTEREST

L'Abbaye de Royaumont, Asnières-sur-Oise, 30km (18 miles) north of Paris. A beautifully preserved Cistercian abbey, founded by the saintly king Louis in 1228.

Musée de la Photographie, Bièvres *(RER C to Massy-Palaiseau, then bus 2002 to Serinet)*. A Frenchman invented photography. This vast, exhaustive collection is a suitable tribute.

OTHER SIGHTS
Fontainebleau ★★★

60km (37½ miles) south-east of Paris (SNCF from Gare de Lyon to Fontainebleau-Avon, then bus A or B)

Louis the Fat (1108–37) first declared this area a royal hunting preserve and a vast and exceptionally beautiful forest still surrounds the little town. In 1527, however, François I demolished the old fortress and commissioned the architect Gilles le Breton to build him the delightful Renaissance château which is the prime attraction. A favourite palace for generations of rulers, almost every future monarch added, demolished and altered bits of it. During the Revolution, it was stripped bare, the canal was drained and the fish were sold to the masses. Nevertheless, it is one of the most charming palaces in France, with a real sense of history and continuity. Napoleon loved Fontainebleau and spent much of his time here. He signed his abdication on 6 April 1814 in the dramatically named Cour des Adieux. The **Musée Napoléon I** concentrates on his daily life.

The beautiful cathedral of Chartres is justly famed for its fine stained-glass windows, especially for the clear 'Chartres blue' colour.

Chartres ★★

85km (53 miles) south-west of Paris (SNCF from Gare Montparnasse to Chartres)

Like Notre Dame, the magnificent cathedral at Chartres stands on ground sacred to many religions over thousands of years. The earliest Christian church was built in the 4th century. It became a major pilgrimage centre in 876 when Charlemagne's grandson presented the Sancta Camisia, supposedly the cloth worn by Mary while giving birth to Christ. The crypt of the existing cathedral dates to 1024, while the spectacular Gothic

OTHER CHATEAUX

Dampierre, *Dampierre-en-Yvelines, 36km (21 miles) south-west of Paris*. A digni-fied 17th-century brick and stone château, surrounded by formal flower gardens.
Ecouen *20km (12¹/₂ miles) north of Paris (metro Line 13 to St-Denis Porte de Paris, then bus 268C, or SNCF from Gard du Nord to Ecouen-Ezanville)*. A supremely ele-gant early 16th-century château, which now houses the lavish **Musée Nationale de la Renaissance**.
Milly-la-Forêt, *55km (35 miles) south of Paris*. The highlight is the nearby **Château de Courances**, with its magnificent 17th-century gardens, but the delightful village has several small exhibitions dedicated to local painters (Rousseau, Decamps, Daubigny and Millet) and an audio-visual on the poet Jean Cocteau.

ECLIPSING THE SUN

In 1661 Fouquet invited the Sun King and court to a grand fête to celebrate the opening of his superb new château, Vaux-le-Vicomte. Louis became so sick with jealousy that he arrested its owner, stripped him of office, possessions and title and exiled him for life. He then set to work to build some-thing much bigger and bet-ter; the result was Versailles.

church, soaring above the little town, was built in the early 13th century. Above all, it has over 150 peerless 13th-century stained-glass windows, telling stories of heroes and the Bible, showing the lives of peasants and princes, honouring God, the saints and the people who paid for them in a unique record of medieval life and thought. Even the local merchants donated 42 windows, each showing the speciality of the guild. The narrow streets around the cathedral have many delightful half-timbered buildings, several other fine churches and a Musée des Beaux-Arts.

St-Germain-en-Laye *
18km (11 miles) west of Paris (RER Line A)
The first castle on this wooded site overlooking the Seine was built in 1124. The earliest surviving building is St Louis' delicate 13th-century Sainte-Chapelle. The surviv-ing château, the work of François I, belongs to the Renaissance, but there was another later version built by Philibert d'Orme in 1557, of which only the Pavillon Henri IV remains. Louis XIV was born here, escaped back here from the mob during the Fronde rebellion and set up court for nearly 40 years, until Versailles was complete. Since 1855 the château has been home to the **Musée des Antiquités Nationale**, the national archaeology collection. The former 17th-century Hôpital Général Royal, *2bis rue Maurice Denis*, now houses the important **Musée Maurice Denis**, dedicated to the artist and his friends, with works by Gauguin, Bonnard, Vuillard, Mondrian and Lalique.

Vaux-le-Vicomte *
Maincy, 50km (30 miles) south-east of Paris (SNCF from Gare de Lyon to Melun, then a taxi)
This magnificent château was built by Le Vau for Louis XIV's finance minister, Fouquet, in 1661. The entire pro-ject was undertaken in five years. Lavishly ornamented, with frescoes by Le Brun in the Grand Salon, and fine gardens by Le Nôtre, it is acknowledged to be one of the finest châteaux in the Ile de France and one of the major architectural influences on Versailles.

Chantilly *

35km (20 miles) north of Paris (SNCF from Gare du Nord to Chantilly)

Two Renaissance châteaux stand side by side in magnificent gardens, laid out in 1662 by Le Nôtre. The décor and furnishings are dazzling, but the prize exhibit is the priceless 15th-century illuminated manuscript, *Les Très Riches Heures du Duc de Berry*. Chantilly also has one of the premier racecourses in France.

Giverny *

80km (50 miles) west of Paris (SNCF from Gare St Lazare to Vernon, then a taxi)

Claude Monet, arguably the greatest of all the Impressionists, lived in this simple house, still crammed with his memorabilia, from 1883 until he died in 1926, creating the luxuriant garden which he then painted and repainted, above all in his most famous series, *Les Nymphéas* (Waterlilies), his canvases becoming bigger and more abstract as he gradually lost his sight.

Thoiry

40km (25 miles) west of Paris (SNCF from Gare de Montparnasse to Montfort l'Amaury, then a bus or taxi)

There is something for everyone here, with a finely furnished château, built in 1564, and now also housing the **Musée des Archives**, 100ha (250 acres) of beautiful gardens with areas of both formal French patterning and English-style parkland, an extensive wildlife park with lions, tigers, elephants and bears, along with gentler creatures and birds, a toy road train and park for miniature animals.

AUVERS-SUR-OISE

40km (25 miles) north-west of Paris (RER Line A to Cergy-Préfecture, then a shuttle bus)

This delightful village was beloved by many Impressionist painters including Pissarro, Corot, Daubigny and Renoir. Here you can visit Van Gogh's grave and the room where he died in 1890. A sophisticated multimedia tour, dedicated to the lives and works of these great artists, is housed in the 17th-century Château d'Auvers.

Monet used his water garden at Giverny as subject matter for many paintings, in particular his magnificent waterlily series.

Paris at a Glance

Office du Tourisme et des Congrès de Paris, 127 avenue des Champs-Elysées, 8th; tel: 49 52 53 54 (metro: Etoile/George V). Open 09:00–20:00 daily. Everything you need under one roof. Other tourist information desks at the **Mairie de Paris** (29 rue de Rivoli, 4th; tel: 42 76 43 43; metro: Hôtel de Ville) and at the **Gare du Nord** (tel: 45 26 94 82); **Gare d'Austerlitz** (tel: 46 07 17 73); **Gare de Lyon** (tel: 43 43 33 24); **Gare Montparnasse** (tel: 43 22 19 19); and in summer only, by the **Eiffel Tower** (tel: 45 51 22 15; metro: Bir Hakeim).
24-hour recorded **English-language information**, tel: 49 52 53 56.

Paris has an excellent public transport network – made up of the metro, buses, both run by RATP, the RER and suburban mainline rail services, run by SNCF.

Tickets
Use same tickets on all transport. Paris is divided into 8 concentric zones; clip more tickets if you are travelling further. Single tickets are expensive, buy a *carnet* of 10 for a 40 per cent discount. Cheaper still are various passes – the 1 day **Formule** 1; 3–5 day **Paris Visite**; and weekly (Mon–Sun) or monthly (from 1st of month) **Carte Orange** (ID

and passport photos required). The cost goes up with the number of zones included (most major sights are within Zones 1–3; Versailles, Disneyland and the airports are in Zone 5).

All tickets are available at main metro, RER and SNCF stations; Formule 1 and *carnets* at some tabacs; Paris Visite and Formule 1 at the main tourist office and airports. **RATP** have two tourist offices at 53bis, quai des Grands Augustins, 6th; tel: 40 46 42 17 (metro: St-Michel); and place de la Madeleine, 1st; tel: 40 06 71 45 (metro: Madeleine). RATP information, tel: 43 46 14 14.

Maps
Le Petit Plan de Paris is an excellent, free transport map. Several department stores sponsor good, free street maps. *Paris par Arrondissement* (pub. Editions l'Indispensable) is the best of several more detailed street atlases, sold in bookshops and news stalls.

The Metro
The metro has numerous stations and trains run every cou-

ple of minutes from about 05:30–01:00. Lines are numbered and colour coded on maps, but are named according to the last stop on the line. To change lines, trace the route to the last stop in the right direction and follow the *Correspondance* sign.

The RER
A cross of four suburban rail lines, A, B, C and D. Few stops in the centre and most useful for longer journeys.

Buses
Good services during the day, either stopping or tailing off after 20:30 and on Sunday. Bus routes and zones are displayed at bus stops and on the sides of the buses. You may have to use more than one ticket for a journey. Put single tickets through the punch machine as you board. *Do not* put your pass through the machine – just show it to the driver.

Restricted night bus service (Noctambus): 01:00–05:00, with 10 lines fanning out from Châtelet (avenue Victoria or rue Saint-Martin) to the surburbs. One bus an hour each way on each route.

PARIS	J	F	M	A	M	J	J	A	S	O	N	D
AV. MAX TEMP. °C	6	7	12	16	20	23	25	24	21	16	10	7
AV. MIN TEMP. °C	1	1	4	6	10	13	15	14	12	8	5	2
AV. MAX TEMP. °F	43	45	54	60	68	73	76	75	70	60	50	44
AV. MIN TEMP. °F	34	34	39	43	49	55	58	58	53	46	40	36
RAINFALL mm	56	46	35	42	57	54	59	64	55	50	51	50
RAINFALL in	2.2	1.8	1.4	1.7	2.2	2.1	2.3	2.5	2.2	2	2	2
Days of Rainfall	17	14	12	13	12	12	12	13	13	13	15	16

Paris at a Glance

Taxis
Plentiful, with 487 taxi ranks. Street hailing is allowed, but rarely successful. Licensed taxis show a white rooflight if available, an orange one if occupied. Three price bands – from 07:00 to 19:00; from 19:00 to 07:00; and a higher charge for night trips to the surburbs. Also supplements at stations, Air France terminals, for luggage, more than three passengers and animals. Avoid unofficial taxis, which charge what they like. 24hr telephone bookings: **Alpha**, tel 45 85 85 85; **Artaxi**, tel 42 41 50 50; **G7**, tel 47 39 47 39; **Taxi Bleu**, tel 49 36 10 10.

Where to Stay

Paris accommodation covers every range, but none of it is cheap. Most places charge per room, not per person. Book ahead during peak seasons (spring and autumn). Check whether cheaper hotels take credit cards.

Accommodation Bureaux
Paris Séjour Reservation, 90 av des Champs-Elysees, 8th; tel: 42 56 30 00 (*metro: George V*). Hotels and self-catering apartments.
Bed & Breakfast 1, 73 rue Notre-Dame-des-Champs, 6th; tel: 43 25 43 97 (*metro: Vavin, Notre Dame-des-Champs*). Bed and breakfast and self-catering apartments.
Tourisme chez l'Habitant, 27 rue Rambuteau, 1st; tel:

42 71 47 47 (*metro: Rambuteau, Les Halles*). Bed and breakfast; minimum stay 2 nights.
  The main **tourist office** has a hotels reservation desk. Almost all major international chains have at least one hotel in the city. The French **Accor Group** (Formule, Novotel, Mercure, Ibis and Sofitel chains) has 29 properties in Paris; tel: 60 87 44 01, while **Timhotel** has 10; tel: 44 15 81 15.

Palace Hotels
These few hotels are so famous and plushy they are tourist attractions in their own right. All very expensive.
Le Bristol, 112 rue du Faubourg St-Honoré, 8th; tel: 42 66 91 45 (*metro: Champs-Elysées-Clemenceau*).
Le Crillon, 10 place de la Concorde, 8th; tel: 42 65 24 24 (*metro: Concorde*).
George V, 31 av George V, 8th; tel: 47 23 54 00 (*metro: George V*).
The Intercontinental, 3 rue de Castiglione, 1st; tel: 44 77 11 11 (*metro: Tuileries, Concorde*).
The Plaza Athenée, 25 av Montaigne, 8th; tel: 47 23 78 33 (*metro: Franklin D. Roosevelt*).
The Ritz, 15 place Vendôme, 1st; tel: 42 60 38 30 (*metro: Tuileries*).

Youth Accommodation
Fédération Unie des Auberges de Jeunesse, 27

rue Pajol, 18th tel: 46 07 00 01 (*metro: Porte de la Chapelle*). Youth hostels affiliated to Hostelling International.
Acceuil des Jeunes en France, 119 rue Saint-Martin, 4th tel: 42 77 87 80 (*metro: Châtelet-Les-Halles, Rambuteau*). Over 5000 cheap beds across Paris for 18–30 year olds.

The Islands
A wonderful area – central yet peaceful and well situated for food, evening strolls and sightseeing.
Luxury
Jeu de Paume, 54 rue St-Louis-en-l'Ile, 4th; tel: 43 26 14 18 (*metro: Pont Marie, Sully Morland*). A 17th-century jeu de paume (early tennis) court now oozing discreet luxury.
Deux Iles, 59 rue St-Louis-en-l'Ile, 4th; tel 43 26 13 35 (*metro: Pont Marie, Sully Morland*). A charmingly converted 17th-century mansion.
Budget
Henri IV, 25 place Dauphine, Ile de la Cité, 1st; tel: 43 54 44 53 (*metro: Cité*). Very simple and very popular.

Beaubourg, Les Halles, The Marais and Bastille
An excellent area with numerous small hotels – central, pleasant for strolling and filled with charming eateries.
Luxury
Pavillon de la Reine, 28 place des Vosges, 3rd; tel: 42 77 96 40 (*metro: Chemin*

Paris at a Glance

Vert, St Paul). Small, elegant courtyard mansion rebuilt to original plans in one of the city's most beautiful squares.
La Bretonnerie, 22 rue Ste-Croix-de-la-Bretonnerie, 4th; tel: 48 87 77 63 (*metro: Hôtel de Ville*). Small, comfortable 17th-century hotel, furnished with antiques.
Mid-range
St Merry, 78 rue de la Verrerie, 4th; tel: 42 78 14 15 (*metro: Hôtel de Ville*). 17th-century presbytery and 19th-century brothel, stylishly converted and furnished with Gothic bric-à-brac.
Budget
Castex, 5 rue Castex, 4th; tel: 42 72 31 52 (*metro: Bastille*). Popular, cheap and cheerful.

Montmartre and the North-East

A little way out, but perfect for those on a moderate budget, with vibrant nightlife. Many cheap hotels, especially near the stations, some handling rough trade
Luxury
Terrass, 12 rue Joseph-de-Maistre, 18th; tel: 46 06 72 85 (*metro: Blanche*). Charmingly decorated, a good restaurant and excellent views.
Mid-range
Prima-Lépic, 29 rue Lépic, 18th; tel: 46 06 44 64 (*metro: Abbesses*). Bright and airy town house hotel in the heart of Montmartre.
Budget
du Marché, 6 passage du

Marché Saint-Martin, 10th; tel: 42 06 44 53 (*metro: Strasbourg St Denis, Château d'Eau*). Simple, comfortable, slightly off the beaten track, but very cheap.

The Louvre and Opéra

Convenient but uninspiring area. Excellent for shopping, lousy for nightlife, although the palace hotels near the Louvre create their own glamour .
Luxury
Régina, 2 place des Pyramides, 1st; tel: 42 60 31 10 (*metro: Tuileries*). Delightful Art Deco building filled with antiques, which often doubles as a film set.
Tuileries, 10 rue St-Hyacinthe, 1st; tel: 42 61 04 17 (*metro: Tuileries*)
Mid-range
Gaillon-Opéra, 9 rue Gaillon, 2nd; tel: 47 42 47 74 (*metro: Opéra, Quatre Septembre*). Warmly welcoming 19th-century building with wooden beams and flowery curtains.

North-West Paris: The Rive Droite

Home to some of the finest hotels in Paris, dripping with money and celebrities. Nightlife centred on the Champs-Elysées. Not for those on a tight budget.
Luxury
Balzac, 6 rue Balzac, 8th; tel: 45 61 97 22 (*metro: George V*). Small, discreet, but extremely luxurious, with an excellent restaurant.

Résidence Lord Byron, 5 rue Châteaubriand, 8th; tel: 43 59 89 98 (*metro: George V*). Pleasant small courtyard hotel.
The Mayflower, next door, is under the same management.

The Eiffel Tower, Les Invalides and the Musée d'Orsay

Fairly quiet and sober, this area is still splendidly central and prices are considerably lower than across the river.
Luxury
Duc de St-Simon, 14 rue de St-Simon, 7th; tel: 45 48 35 66 (*metro: Bac*). Elegant, welcoming hotel round a small, flourishing garden.
Mid-range
Le Pavillon, 54 rue St-Dominique, 7th; tel: 45 51 42 87 (*metro: Invalides, Solférino*). Former convent, with tiny rooms, abundant charm and a central courtyard.
Thoumieux, 79 rue St-Dominique, 7th; tel: 47 05 49 75 (*metro: Invalides, Solférino*). 10 comfortable, but simply furnished rooms, attached to a lively bistro.

The Rive Gauche and Montparnasse

Lively and entertaining area with numerous comfortable, middle-of-the-range hotels and wall-to-wall restaurants. An excellent place to stay.
Luxury
L'Hôtel Guy-Louis-Duboucheron, 13 rue des

Paris at a Glance

Beaux-Arts, 6th; tel: 43 25 27 22 (*metro: St-Germain-des-Prés*). Oscar Wilde died here 'beyond his means' in 1900. The hotel has come a long way since then. Everywhere there is beautiful furniture and a general air of extravagance. Renovated in 1968, each room has its own story. Room 16 is a reconstruction of Oscar Wilde's; room 36 has Art Deco furniture belonging to music hall artist Mistinguett.

Hotel d'Angleterre, 44 rue Jacob, 6th; tel: 42 60 34 72 (*metro: St-Germain-des-Prés*). Once the British Embassy, later Hemingway's home, the treaty which ended the American War of Independence was prepared in this 18th-century building, although it was actually signed further up the street, as Franklin refused to set foot on British soil. The hotel is charming, comfortable, and peaceful, surrounding a small flower-filled courtyard.

Ste-Beuve, 9 rue Ste-Beuve, 6th; tel: 45 48 20 07 (*metro: Notre-Dame des Champs, Vavin*). Small hotel successfully mingling cool, understated elegance and a cosy, welcoming atmosphere.
Mid-range

Welcome Hotel, 66 rue de Seine, 6th; tel: 46 34 24 80 (*metro: Odéon*). Warm and friendly hotel on a lively street, overlooking Buci flower market.

Esméralda, 4 rue St-Julien-le-Pauvre, 5th; tel: 43 54 19 20 (*metro: St-Michel*). Small 16th-century hotel with charmingly eccentric decor.

The Ile de France

Disneyland Paris, Marne-la-Vallée/Chessy, 6 huge theme hotels and a self-catering complex on site. For details and booking for all, tel: 60 30 60 53 or, in the UK, 0171 753 2900.

WHERE TO EAT

Paris has more restaurants per head than any other city in the world. The following list is a minute fragment of the wonderful options available. As well as the individual restaurants, travellers on a moderate budget should look at some of the chains of brasseries, such as **Hippopotamus** and the more upmarket **Brasserie Flo** chain; the Italian **Il Teatro** chain (with seven branches); the many **Batifol** bistros; and the **Bistrot de l'Etoile** and **Bistrot d'A-Côté** chains, which are both cheaper eateries managed by some of the city's great chefs. See also pages 26-29.

The Islands

Auberge de la Reine Blanche, 30 rue St-Louis-en-l'Ile, 4th; tel: 46 33 07 87 (*metro: Pont Marie*). Charming and friendly little restaurant decorated with dolls house furniture. Moderate.

Au Franc Pinot, 1 quai de Bourbon, 4th; tel: 43 29 46 98 (*metro: Pont Marie*). Excellent traditional cellar restaurant and ground floor wine bar. Moderate to expensive.

Au Monde des Chimères, 69 rue St-Louis-en-l'Ile, 4th; tel: 43 54 45 27 (*metro: Pont Marie*). Charming, rather rustic family bistro, serving traditional French food. Moderate.

Le Vieux Bistro, 14 rue du Cloître Notre Dame, 4th; tel: 43 54 18 95 (*metro: Cité*). The honourable exception to the normal lack of quality on the Ile de la Cité. Traditional French cooking in a warm friendly atmosphere. Moderate.

Brasserie de l'Ile St Louis, 55 quai de Bourbon, 4th; tel: 43 54 02 59 (*metro: Pont Marie*). Well-established, relaxed brasserie specializing in food from Alsace. Moderate.

Berthillon, 31 rue St-Louis-en-l'Ile, 4th; tel: 43 54 31 61 (*metro: Pont Marie*). Said to produce the best ice cream in France. About 60 different flavours, also sold in nearby cafés to cut the queues.

Beaubourg, Les Halles, The Marais and Bastille

L'Ambroisie, 9 place des Vosges, 4th; tel: 42 78 51 45 (*metro: St Paul, Chemin Vert*). A magnificent Michelin 3-star restaurant, in a superb setting. Book one month ahead. Very expensive.

Paris at a Glance

Au Pied de Cochon, 6 rue Coquillière, 1st; tel: 42 36 11 75 (*metro: Les Halles*). A huge Paris institution, open 24hr. Set up originally to serve hearty fare to market workers, now the place to come for a breakfast of pig's trotters and onion soup after a heavy night out. Moderate.

Brasserie Bofinger, 5 rue de la Bastille, 4th; tel: 42 72 87 82 (*metro: Chemin Vert*). Seafood specialist, with a 100-year pedigree and delightful art nouveau décor. Moderate.

Chicago Meatpackers, 8 rue Coquillière, 1st; tel:40 28 02 33 (*metro: Les Halles*). Ribs and T-bones for homesick Americans.

La Guirlande de Julie, 25 place des Vosges, 3rd; tel: 48 87 94 07 and **Coconnas**, 2bis place des Vosges, 4th; tel: 42 78 58 16 (*metro: St Paul, Chemin Vert*). Two charming, affordable restaurants, serving classic French cuisine, under the supervision of Claude Terrail of the famous Tour d'Argent.

Jo Goldenberg, 7 rue des Rosiers, 4th; tel: 48 87 20 16 (*metro: St Paul*). The best Jewish deli and restaurant in Paris.

Miravile, 72 quai de l'Hôtel de Ville, 4th; tel: 42 74 72 22 (*metro: Hôtel de Ville*). Cool and elegant restaurant with exquisite food, with a strong emphasis on Provençale cuisine. Book well ahead. Very expensive.

Montmartre and the North-East

A. Beauvilliers, 52 rue Lamarck, 18th; tel: 42 54 54 42 (*metro: Lamarck Caulaincourt*). Grandiose, gilded dining rooms, an open terrace and the finest gourmet cuisine in Montmartre. Expensive.

Brasserie Webler, 14 place de Clichy, 18th; tel: 45 22 53 24 (*metro: Place Clichy*). Try the seafood at this 100-years-old brasserie. Moderate.

Haynes, 3 rue Clauzel, 9th; tel: 48 78 40 63 (*metro: St-Georges*). One of the first American restaurants, with a jazz theme and spicy soul food. Cheap.

Le Restaurant, 32 rue Verou, 18th; tel: 42 23 06 22 (*metro: Blanche, Abbesses*). Bright and cheerful, with an imaginative, modern menu. Moderate.

Le Sagittaire, 77 rue Lamarck, 18th; tel: 42 55 17 40 (*metro: Lamarck Caulaincourt*). Small homely cheerful restaurant serving a well-cooked traditional menu at very affordable prices. There are numerous cafés, bars and restaurants surrounding the famous Place du Tertre. Most serve perfectly adequate food, but prices are way over the top.

The Louvre and Opéra

A la Grille Saint-Honoré, 15 place du Marché St-Honoré, 1st; tel: 46 61 00 93 (*metro: Tuileries*). Excellent little restaurant specializing in game. Moderate.

Angelina, 228 rue de Rivoli, 1st; tel: 42 60 82 00 (*metro: Tuileries*). Ultimate chic, a gilded tea room oozing with 19th-century charm. Expensive.

Chartier, 7 rue du Faubourg-Montmartre, 9th; tel: 47 70 86 29 (*metro: Rue-Montmartre*). A cavernous barn set up in 1892 by the Communist Party to feed workers cheaply. Still offering good, cheap food, appalling service and spectacular Belle Epoque décor.

Country Life, 6 rue Daunou, 2nd; tel: 42 97 48 51 (*metro: Opéra*). A rarity in Paris – a good, cheap vegetarian restaurant.

Fellini, 47 rue Arbre-Sec, 1st, tel: 42 60 90 66 (*metro: Louvre*) Elegant and imaginative, specializing in Italian regional cuisine. Moderate.

Le Grand Colbert, 4 rue Vivienne, 2nd; tel: 42 86 87 88 (*metro: Bourse*). A charming, classic brasserie first opened in 1830 and popular with the theatrical crowd. Open late. Expensive.

Willi's Wine Bar, 13 rue des Petits-Champs, 1st; tel: 42 61 05 09 (*metro: Bourse, Palais-Royal*). English-run wine bar with pleasant décor, good wine list and interesting menu. Moderate.

Also in this area are several palace hotels with superb dining rooms, amongst them the **Ritz**, **Inter-Continental**,

Paris at a Glance

and the **Meurice** (see Hotels, on page 114).

North-West Paris: The Rive Droite
Chicago Pizza Pie Factory, 5 rue de Berri, 8th; tel: 45 62 50 23 (metro: George V). American pizzas and razmatazz. Moderate.

Fauchon–Le30, 30 place de la Madeleine, 8th; tel: 47 42 56 58 (metro: Madeleine). There are several eateries, from café to self-service to grand restaurant in this vast temple to food, headquarters of the Fauchon empire. Try the menu, then buy the ingredients. All price ranges.

L'Avenue, 41 av Montaigne, 8th; tel: 40 70 14 91 (metro: Alma Marceau). Art Deco restaurant with Provençale-inspired food, popular with fashion gurus. Moderate–expensive.

La Maison d'Alsace, 39 av des Champs Elysées, 8th; tel: 43 59 44 24 (metro: Franklin D. Roosevelt). Huge, bright and busy brasserie, specializing in Alsatian food.

Lucas Carton, 9 place de la Madeleine, 8th; tel: 42 65 22 90 (metro: Madeleine). Belle Epoque décor, superbly innovative cuisine from chef Alain Senderens, and 3 Michelin stars. Book ahead. Very expensive.

Maxim's, 3 rue Royale, 8th; tel: 42 65 27 94 (metro: Concorde). A Paris institution for nearly a century, the building is a national monument,

the classic cuisine superb and the live music sophisticated. Book ahead. Very expensive.

This is the natural home of haute cuisine with a cluster of superb, vastly expensive restaurants, including **Chiberta**, **Laurent**, **Ledoyen**, **Taillevent**, and palace hotel dining rooms, amongst them the **Crillon**, **George V**, **Plaza Athénée**, and **Royal Monceau** (see Hotels, on page 114).

The Eiffel Tower, Les Invalides and the Musee d'Orsay
Jules Verne, 2nd floor of the Eiffel Tower, 7th; tel: 45 55 61 44 (metro: Bir-Hakeim). The highest restaurant in Paris, and very popular with both tourists and Parisians. Book way ahead. The service is seamless and the traditional food excellent. Expensive.

La Belle France, 1st floor of the Eiffel Tower, 7th; tel: 45 55 20 04 (metro: Bir-Hakeim). The much cheaper little sister of Jules Vernes, with a pleasant, undemanding menu and café service.

La Ferme Saint-Simon, 6 rue St-Simon, 7th; tel: 45 48 35 74 (metro: Rue du Bac). At lunchtime the restaurant is packed with businessmen and members of parliament. The food is copious, delicious, and filling and the atmosphere is lively. Moderate.

Tan Dinh, 60 rue de Verneuil, 7th; tel: 45 44 04 84 (metro: Rue du Bac). Gourmet

Vietnamese food in charming surroundings. Moderate.

Thoumieux, 79 rue St-Dominique, 7th; tel: 47 05 49 75 (metro: Invalides, Solférino). A jolly bistro with hearty, country-style cuisine. Cheap.

The Rive Gauche and Montparnasse
A foodie's mecca, offering anything and everything from the sublime to the hamburger. For the best array of cheap and cheerful places in town, stroll the narrow pedestrianized streets behind **St-Julien-le-Pauvre** or in the area between **Place Saint-André-des-Arts** and **Saint-Germain-des-Prés**.

Brasserie Lipp, 151 boulevard Saint-Germain, 6th; tel: 45 48 53 91 (metro: St-Germain-des-Prés). A famous brasserie whose clientèle has included the rich and famous from Hemingway to Madonna and whose 1920s décor is a national monument. Moderate.

La Brochette, 25 rue Poliveau, 5th; tel: 45 35 44 38 (metro: Saint-Marcel). One of many good tiny family-run restaurants, serving cheap, traditional North African couscous.

La Coupole, 102 boulevard du Montparnasse, 14th; tel: 43 20 14 20 (metro: Vavin). One of the great artists' hangouts of the 1920s and 30s, this huge, bustling brasserie has been cashing in ever since.

Paris at a Glance

La Cour aux Crêpes, 27 rue Galande, 5th; tel: 43 25 45 00 (*metro: Maubert-Mutualité*). One of several excellent, very reasonable crêperies in the area.

Le Bistrot du Dôme, 1 rue Delambre, 14th; tel: 43 35 32 00 (*metro: Vavin*). Simple, charming, popular seafood restaurant. Moderate.

Le Procope, 13 rue de l'Ancienne Comédie, 6th; tel: 43 26 99 20 (*metro: Odéon*). Founded in 1686, this is one of the oldest and most famous cafés in Paris. During the Revolution it became the Café de Zoppi and the drinking haunt of the infamous Marat. Voltaire, Balzac and Verlaine were other habitués. Today visitors come to see the portrait of the infamous Dr Guillotin (yes, that one) and think historical thoughts as they eat. The food is traditional, prices moderate.

La Tour d'Argent, 15-17 quai de la Tournelle, 5th; tel: 43 54 23 31 (*metro: Maubert-Mutualité*). One of the meccas of French gastronomy since 1582, the food is traditional French and about the best you will ever taste – the duck with cherries even comes with a numbered certificate. Book way ahead. Very expensive.

Perraudin, 157 rue Saint-Jacques, 6th; tel: 46 33 15 75 (*RER: Luxembourg*). A totally traditional bistro serving onion soup and boeuf bourguignon to the local students. Cheap.

ENTERTAINMENT

Listings guides: *l'Officiel des Spectacles* and *Pariscope* (8-page English supplement) both available weekly from any newsagent.

English-language hotline; tel: 49 52 53 56.

Half-price ticket kiosks: RER Châtelet-Les Halles, 1st, and at 15 place de la Madeleine, 8th (*metro: Madeleine*). Closed Mon, afternoon only Sun. No credit cards.

Virgin Megastore, 60 av des Champs-Elysées, 8th; tel: 49 53 50 00 (*metro: Franklin D. Roosevelt*). Wide-ranging booking agency handling everything from theatre to rock and sporting events.

You can also book by credit card on Minitel.

Cabaret
Bal du Moulin Rouge, 83 blvd de Clichy, place Blanche, 9th, 75009; tel: 46 06 00 19 (*metro: Blanche*).

Crazy Horse Saloon, 12 av George V, 75008; tel: 47 23 32 32 (*metro: George V*).

Le Lido de Paris, 116bis, av des Champs-Elysées, 75008; tel: 40 76 56 10 (*metro: George V*).

Folies-Bergère, 32 rue Richer, 75009; tel: 44 79 98 98 (*metro: Cadet, Rue Montmartre*).

plus a great many others, most in Montmartre area. Traditional revues with chorus girls in feathers; gay and drag acts; sex shows; stand-up comedy and acid political satire (good French needed). Famous venues are fun, but very expensive.

Theatre and Cinema
For French-speakers, there are numerous theatres, from the traditional to small experimental performance spaces. There are huge numbers of cinemas throughout the city, showing everything from Hollywood blockbusters to retrospectives and art films. VO (Version Originale) means it's subtitled; VF (Version Française) means it's been dubbed.

Comédie Française, place de la Comédie Française, 1st; tel: 40 15 00 15 (*metro: Palais-Royal*). The great classic home of French drama.

Opera and Ballet
Opéra-Bastille, place de la Bastille, 11th; tel: 44 73 13 00 (*metro: Bastille*).

Opéra-Garnier, place de l'Opéra, 2nd; tel: 47 42 53 71 (*metro: Opéra*). Cheap standby tickets on day of performance.

Music
There is always music available – on the streets, in the churches and museums, cafés, clubs and concert halls. **Free classical concerts** held in several churches, including **Notre-Dame**, **St-Merri**, **St-Sulpice**, and **St-Eustache**, museums including the **Musée d'Art Moderne**, the **Musée de l'Homme** and in numerous parks. Look out for

Paris at a Glance

handbills or see listings.

Cité de la Musique, 221 av Jean-Jaurès, 19th; tel: 44 84 44 84 (*metro: Porte Pantin*). Co-ordinates summer classical music festival.

Centre d'Information du Jazz, 21bis rue de Paradis, 10th; tel: 44 83 10 30 (*metro: Château-d'Eau*). Clearing house and information service for everything to do with jazz in Paris.

TOURS

Bus

France Tourisme/Paris Vision: 12 rue de Mogador, 9th; tel: 48 74 45 08 (*metro: Opéra*).

Cityrama: 4 place des Pyramides, 1st; tel: 44 55 61 00 (*metro: Pyramides*).

Paris Bus/Les Cars Rouges: 2hr 15min circuits of Paris, with a guided commentary in French and English. Board or break your journey at any of nine stops; ticket valid for 2 days. 3/5 rue Talma, 16th; tel: 42 30 55 50 (*metro: La Muette*).

Boat

Bâteaux Mouches: every 30min, 10:00–23:00, from the Right Bank, Pont de l'Alma (*metro: Alma Marceau*); tel: booking – 42 25 96 10, information – 40 76 99 99. Largest and best known of the sightseeing boats. Commentaries in French, German and English. Lunch (13:00), and dinner cruises (20:30).

Bâteaux Parisiens: every 30min, 10:00–23:00 summer, 10:00–18:00 winter, from Port de la Bourdonnais, Pont d'Iéna, 7th (*metro: Bir Hakeim/Trocadéro*) and Quai de Montebello, 5th (*metro: Maubert-Mutualité/St-Michel*); tel: 44 11 33 33. Lunch (12:15) and dinner cruises (20:30).

Vedettes de Paris: every 30min, 10am–12 noon, and 1.30–18:30/19:00, from the Square du Vert Galant, Ile de la Cité (*metro: Cité*) and Port de Suffren, Pont d'Iéna (*metro: Bir Hakeim/ Trocadéro*); tel: 47 05 71 29/46 33 98 38. Some evening trips, 21–22:30. Discounts for Paris Visite ticket holders.

Batobus: unguided water bus service, every 36min. 5 stops at the Eiffel Tower, Musée d'Orsay, the Louvre, Notre Dame and the Hôtel de Ville. April–Oct only, 10:00–c19:00, tel: 44 11 33 44.

Canal trips

Paris Canal: 3hr cruise on the Seine and Canal Saint-Martin. 1 per day each way, 2 on weekends and public holidays. Quai Anatole France, Musée d'Orsay (*RER: Musée d'Orsay*) and Parc de La Villette, *19/21 quai de la Loire, 19th*; tel: 42 40 96 97 (*metro: Jaurès*).

Canauxrama: 3hr cruise on the Canal Saint Martin. 2 departures each way daily. Port de l'Arsenal, *opp. 50 blvd de la Bastille, 12th (metro: Quai de la Rapée*); the Bassin de la Villette, *5bis quai de la Loire, 19th*; tel: 42 39 15 00 (*metro: Jaurès*).

Paris on Two Wheels
Several companies offer bicycle rental and guided tours for the brave.

Paris Bike: 2 and 4hr tours of Paris, the Bois de Boulogne and Versailles with English-speaking guide. Reserve 48hr in advance. 83 rue Daguerre, 14th, tel: 45 38 58 58 (*metro: Denfert-Rochéreau*).

Mountain Bike Trip: 6 place Etienne Pernet, 15th, tel: 48 42 57 87 (*metro: Félix Faure*).

Paris à vélo c'est sympa!: 9 rue Jacques-Coeur, 4th; tel: 48 87 60 01 (*metro: Bastille*). Rental and half-day guided tours.

SIGHTSEEING

Few sights are free, and tickets can be expensive. Buy a ticket for one leg, or whole circuit. Occasional discounts of up to 50 per cent for ISIC (international student) cards or Paris Visite tickets. The best option is to buy a **Carte Inter-Musée**. This 1, 3 or 5 day pass gives entry to 65 different monuments and museums, including all the most famous. Recoup the cost in 3–4 visits and avoid horrendous queues at major sights. On sale at all participating museums and monuments, tourist offices and main metro stations.

Paris at a Glance

Shopping

Haute Couture

On avenue Montaigne (*metro: Franklin D. Roosevelt or Alma-Marceau*): 2, **Emanuel Ungaro**; 17-19, **Hanae Mori** and **Valentino**; 26, **Christian Lacroix**; 29, **Guy Laroche** ; 30, **Christian Dior**; 39, **Nina Ricci**; 40, **Per Spook**; 42, **Chanel**; 49, **Thierry Mugler**; 51, **Jean-Louis Scherrer**; 52, **Jil Sander**; 57, **Escada**.

On av. George V (*metro: Alma-Marceau*): 8, **Boutique Givenchy**; 10, **Balenciaga**.

On rue du Faubourg-St-Honoré, (*metro: Champs Elysées-Clemenceau*): 19, **Karl Lagerfeld**; 25, **Balmain**; 59, **Pierre Cardin**; 62, **Versace**; 88, **Louis Feraud**.

On rue François 1er (*metro: Franklin D. Roosevelt*): 31, **Carven**; 35, **Ted Lapidus**; 44, **Pierre Balmain**; 62, **Philippe Venet**.

Elsewhere:

Paco Rabanne, 23 rue du Cherche Midi, 6th; (*metro: St Sulpice*).

Torrente, 1 rond-point des Champs-Elysées, 8th; (*metro: Franklin D. Roosevelt*). **Yves St Laurent**, 5 av Marceau, 16th; (*metro: Alma-Marceau*).

Prêt-à-porter

Many famous couture houses have cheaper ready-to-wear showrooms on the Left Bank. Those after even greater bargains should look for *dégriffé* signs. These denote designer products with the original label cut out, which are sold off at vast discounts due to overproduction or slight shop soiling. Good hunting grounds include Rue Saint-Placid, Rue des Saints-Pères, Boulevard Saint-Michel, and Rue du Vieux Colombier. Rue Bonaparte is **the** shopping street of the Left Bank, but lock up your credit cards and window shop.

English Language Bookshops

Albion, 13 rue Charles V, 4th; tel: 42 72 50 71 (*metro: St Paul*).

Brentano's, 7 av de l'Opéra, 2nd; tel: 42 61 52 50 (*metro: Opéra*)

Galignani's, 224 rue de Rivoli, 1st; tel: 42 60 76 07 (*metro: Tuileries*)

Shakespeare & Co, 37 rue de la Bûcherie, 5th; tel: 43 26 96 50 (*metro: Saint-Michel*).

WH Smith, 248 rue de Rivoli, 1st; tel: 44 77 88 99 (*metro: Concorde*).

Tea and Tattered Pages, 24 rue Mayet, 6th; tel: 40 65 94 35 (*metro: Duroc*).

Village Voice, 6 rue Princesse, 6th; tel: 46 33 36 47 (*metro: Mabillon*)

Fleas, Stamps and Car Boots

As well as its many delectable food markets (see page 90), Paris also has a thriving collection of specialist markets. Stamp collectors should head for the **Marché aux Timbres**, cour Marigny, 8th (*metro: Champs-Elysées-Clemenceau*); open Thurs, Sat and Sun. Those after prints and second-hand books should trawl the many stalls along the quays, on both sides of the river, near the Ile de la Cité (*metro: Châtelet, St Michel*); open daily. Grand-daddy of all the local flea markets, selling anything antique or merely second hand, including clothes, is at **Saint Ouen** (*metro: Saint-Ouen, Clignancourt*); open Sat–Mon. There are others, smaller, less touristy and with perhaps a remote chance of a bargain, at the **Porte de Vanves**, av Georges-Lafenestre and av Marc-Sangier (*metro: Porte-de-Vanves*); open Sat and Sun; and the **Porte de Montreuil**, 93 Montreuil (*metro: Porte-de-Montreuil*); open Sat–Mon.

The Perfect Picnic

Poilâne, 8 rue du Cherche-Midi, 6th, is reckoned by many to be the best bakery in Paris. The speciality is a large country loaf that has become so popular that it is known everywhere as a *poilâne*. At **Beatrix**, 42 rue Dauphine, 6th, the speciality is baguettes cooked in a proper wood-burning oven.

For charcuterie, try **Au Cochon d'Auvergne**, 48 rue Monge, 5th, and, in the 6th, **Charles**, 10 rue Dauphine and **Coesnon**, 30 rue Dauphine. For cheese, go to **Barthélémy**, 51 rue de Grenelle, 7th and for absolutely everything, wallow in glorious food at **Fauchon**, 26 place de la Madeleine, 8th.

Travel Tips

French Tourist Offices Abroad

Australia: 12 Castlereagh St, Sydney NSW 2000, tel: 02-231 5244; fax: 02-221 8682.
Canada: 1981 Avenue McGill College, Ste 490, Montreal, Quebec H3A 2W9, tel: (514) 288 4264; fax: (514) 845 4868.
30 St Patrick Street, Ste 700, Toronto, Ontario M5T 3A3, tel: (416) 593 6427; fax: (416) 979 7587.
Ireland: 35 Lower Abbey St, Dublin 1, tel: 01-703 4046; fax: 01-874 7324.
South Africa: PO Box 41022, Craighall 2024, tel: 011-880 8062; fax: 011-880 7772.
UK: 178 Piccadilly, London W1V 0AL, tel: 0891-244 123 (premium rate line); fax: 0171-493 6594.
USA: 444 Madison Ave, 16th flr, New York, NY10020, tel: (212) 838 7800; fax: (212) 838 7855.

Getting There
By Air
Flights to Paris from almost every country in the world. Direct scheduled services from most UK regional airports.

Airports
Roissy-Charles de Gaulle, 23km (14 miles) north of Paris on autoroute A1. 24hr flight information, tel: 48 62 22 80. Tourist information and hotel reservation offices, tel: 48 62 27 29, open 07:00–19:00.
Airport transfers: RER line B3, every 15min.

Air France coaches every 15–20min to Place Charles de Gaulle-Etoile and Porte Maillot; tel: 43 23 97 10.

RATP Roissybus services every 15min to Opéra-Garnier, Gare de l'Est, Gare Montparnasse and Nation; tel: 48 04 18 24. Journey time approximately 1hr.
Orly, 20km (12 1/2 miles) south of Paris on autoroute A6. 24hr flight information, tel: 49 75 15 15.

Airport transfers: RER Line C2. Air France coaches every 12min to Les Invalides and Gare Montparnasse; tel: 43 24 97 10. Journey time approximately 35min.

RATP Orlybus every 13min to Place Denfert-Rochereau. RATP information, tel: 43 46 14 14 (06:00–21:00).

By Train
Six main SNCF stations handle services from all France and most other European countries. All are served by metro and RER.
Fares and timetable enquiries for all stations, tel: 30 64 50 50; reservations for all SNCF trains (07:00 - 22:00), tel: 45 65 60 60; other SNCF enquiries, tel: 45 82 50 50.
Paris-Nord, *15 rue de Dunkerque, 10th*; tel: 49 95 10 00. Eurostar services through the Channel Tunnel and some UK boat trains.
Paris-Saint-Lazare, *rue St-Lazare, 8th*; tel: 42 85 88 00. UK boat trains.
Paris-Est, *10 place du 11 novembre 1918, 10th*; tel: 40 18 20 00.
Paris-Montparnasse, *17 blvd de Vaugirard, 6th*; tel: 40 48 10 00.
Paris-Austerlitz, *53 quai d'Austerlitz, 5th*; tel: 45 84 14 18.
Paris-Gare de Lyon, *place Louis Armand, 12th*; tel: 40 19 60 00.

UK Tour Operators
Kirker Europe, 3 New

Concordia Wharf, Mill Street, London SE1 2BB; tel: 0171 231 3333.

Paris Travel Service, Bridge House, Broxbourne, Herts EN10 7DT; tel: 01992 456000.

Time Off, Chester Close, London SW1X 7BQ, tel: 0171-235 8070, or 0171-235 8070 to order a brochure.

All of the above are excellent companies specializing in European city breaks and offering a wide range of Paris options.

Documents

EU and other European, US, Canadian and New Zealand citizens need a current passport. Other nationals may require a visa and should check with their nearest French embassy. Drivers from Europe, North America, Australia and New Zealand can use their national licence; others should get an international licence. A green card is required for all foreign vehicles.

When to go

Anytime. The climate is probably best and Paris looks prettiest in May/June and September/October. These are prime tourist seasons and also the festival seasons. Always make your hotel bookings in advance. Avoid travelling on the last weekends in July and August, the beginning and end of the French school holidays. In August Parisians go to the country, and many of the smaller shops and hotels close, but the town is pleasantly empty.

National Holidays

New Year's Day (1 January), Easter Sunday and Monday, May Day (1 May), VE Day (8 May), Ascension Day, Whit Monday (Pentecost), Bastille Day (14 July), Assumption (15 August), All Saint's Day (1 November), Armistice Day (11 November), Christmas Day.

Communications
Post

Stamps from PTT (Poste et Telecommunications) offices, open Mon–Fri 08:00–19:00, Sat 08:00–12:00, and tabacs. Post boxes are small, wall-mounted and mustard yellow. The main post office, *52 rue du Louvre, 1st*; tel: 40 28 20 00 (*metro: Louvre-Rivoli, Les Halles*) is open 24hr for telephones and collecting *poste restante* mail.

Telephone

Phone boxes use either coins (1–5 franc pieces), credit cards or phone cards, available from tabacs, tourist shops etc. Most boxes handle international calls and have multilingual instructions. Also phone from PTT offices, and many cafés have pay phones (for local calls only). It is possible to use many national charge cards (eg Mercury, BT, AT&T etc) and Call Direct.

To phone Paris from abroad: 33 (France) + 1 (Paris) + number
To phone Paris from provincial France: 16 + 1 + number
To phone provincial France from Paris: 16 + number
To phone abroad, dial 19,

wait for the change of tone, then the country code (GB – 44) and number.

Emergencies

Police – 17
Fire – 18
SAMU (ambulance) – 15
Emergency doctor – 47 07 77 77
Emergency dentist – 43 37 51 00
24hr infirmary – 43 43 25 45
American Hospital – 46 41 25 25
Lost Property Office, *36 rue des Morillons, 15th*, tel: 45 31 14 80 (*metro: Convention*).

Health

EU citizens are entitled to sub-sidized (not totally free) treat-ment. Fill in Form E111 (from DSS offices) before travelling. You will be expected to pay, then claim for reimbursement. Full travel insurance is advisable. France is safe and clean, the water is drinkable and no vaccinations are needed. Pharmacists are often able to treat minor ailments. To find a pharmacy open out of hours, tel: 45 62 02 41.

Dhéry, Galerie des Champs, *84 av des Champs-Elysées, 8th*; tel: 45 62 02 41. 24hr pharmacy.

English-speaking hospitals

British Hospital, 3 rue Barbés, 92300 Levallois, tel: 47 58 13 12.

American Hospital, 63 boulevard Victor-Hugo, 92202, tel: 46 41 25 25. Both private and expensive; most public hospitals will have some English-speaking staff.

Insurance

A good travel insurance policy should cover all medical costs, including repatriation; the loss, theft or damage of any belongings and money; cancellation and delay; and third party damages should you cause an accident. Available from any reputable travel agent.

Safety

Paris is no more or less dangerous than any other major city. There are no real 'no-go' areas, although women should think twice about walking around the Gare du Nord/Pigalle area on their own at night. Otherwise, be sensible. Be careful crossing the roads – the traffic can be lethal. Don't carry all your money and valuables around with you; most hotels can provide a secure lock-up. Men should make sure their wallet is securely anchored in an inside pocket and women should use a handbag with a cross-shoulder strap and zip. Late at night keep to well-lit streets and if in doubt take a taxi.

French Embassies Abroad

Australia: 6 Perth Ave, Yarralumla, Canberra ACT 2600, tel: 06-270 5111; fax: 06-273 3193.

Canada: 42 Promenade Sussex, Ottawa Ontario Q1M 2C9; tel: 613-789 1795; fax: 613-789 0279.

Ireland: 36 Ailesbury Road, Ballsbridge, Dublin 4, tel: 353-01-260 1666; fax: 01-283 0178.

New Zealand: 1 Willeston Street (PO Box 1695) Wellington, tel: 04-472 0200; fax: 04-472 5887.

South Africa: (Jan–Jun) 1009 Main Tower, Cape Town Centre, Heerengracht 8001, Cape Town, tel: 021-212 050/2; fax: 21-261 996. (Jul–Oct) 807 George Avenue, Arcadia, Pretoria 0083, tel: 012-435 564/5; fax: 012-433 481.

UK: 58 Knightsbridge, London SW1X 7JT, tel: 0171-201 1000, fax: 0171-201 1059.

USA: 4101 Reservoir Road, NW, Washington DC 20007, tel: (202) 944 6000; fax: (202) 944 6166.

Embassies and Consulates in Paris

Australia, *4 rue Jean Rey, 15th*; tel: 40 59 33 00 (*metro: Bir Hakeim*).

Canada, *35 av Montaigne, 8th*; tel: 44 43 29 00 (*metro: Franklin D. Roosevelt*).

New Zealand, *7ter rue Léonard-da-Vinci, 16th*; tel: 45 00 24 11 (*metro: Victor Hugo*).

South Africa, *59 quai d'Orsay, 9th*, tel: 45 55 92 37 (*metro: Invalides*).

UK, *35 rue Faubourg St-Honoré, 8th*; tel: 42 66 91 42 (*metro: Concorde*). Consulate: *9 av Hoche, 8th*; tel: 42 66 38 10 (*metro: Charles de Gaulle-Etoile*).

USA, *2 av Gabriel, 8th*; tel: 42 96 12 02 (*metro: Champs Elysées-Clemenceau*). Consulate: *2 rue Saint Florentin, 1st*; tel: 42 96 14 88 (*metro: Concorde*).

Money

The currency is the franc, divided into 100 centimes. Credit cards are widely accepted, but few places other than banks will accept Eurocheques. Central banks open Mon–Fri 09:00–16:30. Some branches open on Sat, but close on Mon; many close 12:00–14:00.

American Express: Main Office, *11, rue Scribe, 9th*; tel: 47 77 70 07 (*metro: Opéra; RER: Auber*). Open Mon–Fri 08:30–18:30, Sat 09:00–17:30. For lost or stolen travellers cheques, tel: 05 90 86 00 (24hr).

Thomas Cook: *8 place de l'Opéra, 9th*; tel: 47 42 46 52

CONVERSION CHART		
FROM	**TO**	**MULTIPLY BY**
Millimetres	inches	0.0394
Metres	yards	1.0936
Metres	feet	3.281
Kilometres	miles	0.6214
Hectares	acres	2.471
Litres	pints	1.760
Kilograms	pounds	2.205
Tonnes	tons	0.984

To convert Celsius to Fahrenheit: $\times 9 \div 5 + 32$

FURTHER READING

Gilles Desmons, *Walking Paris*, New Holland Publishers, London, 1994: Detailed descriptions of 30 walks in and around the city. Anne and Alain Riou (annual), *Paris Pas Cher*, Editions du Seuil, Paris. Excellent listings guide to bargains from theatre tickets to couturier gowns. French. *Guide Gault Millau Paris* (annual). The city's top food and drink listings, also crammed with other useful information. French.
Robert Cole, *A Traveller's History of France*, Windrush London, 1988: Easily digestible history of France from the year dot.
John Ardagh, *France Today*, Penguin, London, 1988: Analysis of modern French society.

Ian Littlewood, *Paris: A Literary Companion*, John Murray, London, 1987: Anthology of great and not-so-great writings on the city. Raymond Rudorff, *Belle Epoque: Paris in the Nineties*, Hamish Hamilton, London, 1972: Gay Paris at the turn of the century. Victor Hugo, *Les Misérables*, Penguin Classics. Social injustice, revolution and a rousing story by the great 19th-century commentator on Paris. George Orwell, *Down and Out in London and Paris*, Penguin, London. Street life during the 1930s depression. Also novels by Honoré de Balzac, Emile Zola and Simone de Beauvoir, mostly available in English translation through Penguin Classics.

(metro: Opéra). Open Mon–Sat 09:00–19:00 ; Sun 10:00–19:00. For lost or stolen travellers cheques, tel: 05 90 83 30 (24hr).

Tipping
Taxi drivers 10 per cent; cinema and theatre usherettes, tour guides 3–5FF. Restaurant prices include all taxes and service charges, so leave small change only for exceptional service.

Electricity
220V, 2 round pin plugs. Sockets are always live, so don't leave things plugged in.

Time
GMT + 1hr in winter; + 2hr in summer.

Toilets
Standards and availability of public toilets have improved greatly over the last 10 years, and most are now squeaky clean. Available in selected metro stations, on the streets in main tourist areas (often space-capsule style) and in all cafés and bars, although you need to be brave to use these if you haven't bought anything. You may have to walk through the gents to reach the ladies. As ever, life is easier for men; women should keep a stash of 1 and 2 franc pieces handy.

Basic Vocabulary
Absolute Basics
Good morning/afternoon *Bonjour*
Good evening/night *Bon soir/bonne nuit*
Goodbye *Au revoir*
Sir (common usage for all men) *Monsieur*
Madam (common usage for all women) *Madame*
Yes *Oui*
No *Non*
OK *D'accord*
Please *S'il vous plaît*
Thank you (very much) *Merci (beaucoup)*
Excuse me/sorry *Pardon*
I don't understand *Je ne comprends pas*
Do you speak English? *Parlez-vous anglais?*
Do you have...? *Avez-vous/Est-ce que vous avez...?*
How much is...? *Combien coûte...?*
When is...? *A quelle heure est...?*
Open *Ouvert*
Closed *Fermé*
Speak more slowly *Parlez plus lentement*
Write it down *Ecrivez-le*
Leave me alone *Laissez-moi tranquille*
Forbidden *Interdit*
Out of service *Hors de service/en panne*
Watch out! *Attention!*
Help! *Au secours/aidez-moi!*

Getting Around
Where is...? *Où est...?*
Left *Gauche*
Right *Droit*
Straight on *Tout droit*
Railway station *La gare*
Metro station *La station de métro*
Bus stop *L'arrêt du bus*

Platform *Le quai*
Ticket *Le billet*
One-way *Simple*
Return *Aller-retour*
Child's ticket *Un billet d'enfant*
Book of tickets *Un carnet*
Street plan *Un plan*
Map *Une carte*

Calendar

Monday *Lundi*
Tuesday *Mardi*
Wednesday *Mercredi*
Thursday *Jeudi*
Friday *Vendredi*
Saturday *Samedi*
Sunday *Dimanche*

January *Janvier*
February *Février*
March *Mars*
April *Avril*
May *Mai*
June *Juin*
July *Juillet*
August *Août*
September *Septembre*
October *Octobre*
November *Novembre*
December *Décembre*

Numbers

Half *Demi/la moitié*
One *Un*
Two *Deux*
Three *Trois*
Four *Quatre*
Five *Cinque*
Six *Six*
Seven *Sept*
Eight *Huit*
Nine *Neuf*
Ten *Dix*
Eleven *Onze*
Twelve *Douze*
Thirteen *Treize*
Fourteen *Quatorze*
Fifteen *Quinze*

Sixteen *Seize*
Seventeen *Dix-sept*
Eighteen *Dix-huit*
Nineteen *Dix-neuf*
Twenty *Vingt*
Thirty *Trente*
Hundred *Cent*
Thousand *Mille*

In the hotel

Floor (as in 2nd floor) *L'étage*
Lift (elevator) *L'ascenseur*
Room *La chambre*
Key *La clef/clé*
(Private) bathroom *La salle de bain (privée)*
Bath *Le bain*
Shower *La douche*
Toilet *La toilette*
(Double) bed *Un (grand) lit*
Pillow *Un oreiller*
Air-conditioning *La climatisation*
Heating *Le chauffage*
... does not work *...ne marche pas.*

Mealtimes

Breakfast (included) *Le petit déjeuner (compris)*
Lunch *Le déjeuner*
Dinner *Le dîner*
Fixed price meal *Le menu*
Dish of the day *Le plat du jour*
Starter *Hors d'oeuvres*
Soup *La soupe*
Main course *L'entrée*
Pudding *Le dessert*
The menu *La carte*
The bill *L'addition*
(Fizzy) Water *L'eau (gazeuse)*
Milk *Le lait*
Fruit juice *Le jus de fruit*
Tea *Le thé*
Herbal tea *Une tisane*
Hot chocolate *Un chocolat chaud*
Coffee *Le café*

Black *Noir*
With cream *Café au lait/café crème*
Wine *Le vin*
Red/white/rosé *Rouge/blanc/rosé*
Bread *Le pain*
Butter *Le beurre*
Meat *La viande*
Beef *Le boeuf*
Pork *Le porc*
Lamb *L'agneau*
Chicken *Le poulet/poussin*
Liver *Le foie*
Kidney *Le rognon*
Sweetbread *Le ris*
Blue (still mooing) *Bleu*
Rare *Saignant*
Medium *A point*
Well-done *Bien cuit*
Fish *Le poisson*
Hake *Le colin*
Trout *La truite*
Prawn *La crevette*
Oyster *La huître*
Snail *L'escargot*
Vegetarian *Végétarien*
Vegetables *Les légumes*
Potato *La pomme de terre*
Chips *Les frites*
Rice *Le riz*
(Green) beans *Les haricots (verts)*
Peas *Les petits pois*
Mixed salad *Une salade mixte*
Tomato *La tomate*
Onion *Un oignon*
Lettuce *La laitue*
Cheese *Le fromage*
Ice-cream *La glace*
Apple *La pomme*
Orange *L'orange*
Lemon *Le citron*
Pear *Le poire*
Peach *La pêche*
Apricot *L'abricot*
Black currant *Le cassis*
Strawberry *La fraise*
Raspberry *La framboise*

INDEX